The
Girls' Guide
TO
CONQUERING LIFE

Other books by Jonathan Catherman

The Manual to Manhood
The Manual to Middle School

The *Girls' Guide* TO CONQUERING LIFE

How to
ACE an Interview,
CHANGE a Tire, **TALK** to a Guy,
and 97 Other **SKILLS** You Need
to Thrive

ERICA AND JONATHAN CATHERMAN

Revell
a division of Baker Publishing Group
Grand Rapids, Michigan

© 2018 by Erica and Jonathan Catherman

Published by Revell
a division of Baker Publishing Group
PO Box 6287, Grand Rapids, MI 49516-6287
www.revellbooks.com

Printed in the United States of America

ISBN 978-0-8007-2980-6 (softcover)

Library of Congress Cataloging in Publication Control Number: 2017061367

The authors are represented by the literary agency of Books & Such.

18   19   20   21   22   23   24   7   6   5   4   3   2   1

In keeping with biblical principles of creation stewardship, Baker Publishing Group advocates the responsible use of our natural resources. As a member of the Green Press Initiative, our company uses recycled paper when possible. The text paper of this book is composed in part of post-consumer waste.

This book is dedicated to:

Linda & LaRelle

Two wonderful mothers.
You are our friends and the women who taught us
how to be strong, kind, loving, and adventurous.

Contents

Introduction   9

1 Guys & Dating   13

How to Talk with a Guy You Like · How to Invite a Guy on a First Date · How to Plan a Date · How to Decide Who Pays on a Date · How to Meet a Guy's Parents for the First Time · How to Balance Time with Boyfriend vs. Girlfriends · How to Respectfully Break Up with a Guy

2 Social Skills & Manners   33

How to Shake Hands · How to Introduce Yourself · How to Introduce Other People · How to Listen Well · How to Speak Up for Yourself or Others · How to Open the Door for Another Person · How to Set a Table · How to Order from a Menu · How to Leave a Tip · How to Wrap a Gift · How to Clean a Bathroom · How to Make a Bed

3 Work & Ethics   67

How to Apply for a Job · How to Fill Out an Application · How to Interview for a Job · How to Ask for a Raise · How to Ask for a Promotion · How to Resign · How to Ask for a Reference

4 Wealth & Money Management   89

How to Create a Personal Budget · How to Build a Savings Account · How to Manage a Credit Card Account · How to Invest in the Future · How to Live Debt-Free

5 Health & Beauty   105

How to Properly Wash Your Hair · How to Shave Your Legs · How to Shave under Your Arms · How to Apply Hair-Styling Product · How to Wash Your Hands Properly · How to Freshen Bad Breath · How to Wear Perfume · How to Wash Your Face · How to Trim Your Fingernails · How to Care for Your Feet · How to Apply Nail Polish

6 Clothes & Fashion   135

How to Wash Laundry · How to Dry Laundry · How to Iron a Button-Down Shirt · How to Iron Slacks/Pants · How to Care for Leather Shoes or Boots · How to Wear a Scarf · How to Sew On a Button · How to Spot Treat a Stain · How to Fold a Shirt · How to Shop for a Bra

7 Sports & Recreation   163

How to Kick a Soccer Ball · How to Set a Volleyball · How to Throw a Football · How to Shoot a Basketball · How to Pitch a Softball · How to Swing a Golf Club · How to Putt · How to Throw Darts · How to Hit a Cue Ball · How to Pitch Horseshoes

8 Cars & Driving   191

How to Shift a Manual Transmission · How to Change a Flat Tire · How to Jump-Start a Dead Battery · How to Check the Oil · How to Parallel Park · How to Behave after an Auto Accident · How to Behave during a Police Stop

9 Food & Cooking   215

How to Make a Grocery List and Stock a Pantry · How to Brew Coffee · How to Make Pancakes from Scratch · How to Scramble Eggs · How to Cook Bacon · How to Boil Pasta · How to Cook Rice · How to Make Mashed Potatoes · How to Oven-Bake a Whole Chicken · How to Broil Steak · How to Pan-Sear Fish · How to Light a Charcoal Grill · How to Grill Steak · How to Grill Pork Chops · How to Sharpen a Kitchen Knife

10 Tools & Fix-It   255

How to Stock a Tool Kit · How to Read a Tape Measure · How to Swing a Hammer · How to Cut with a Circular Saw · How to Use a Drill · How to Use a Crowbar · How to Use an Adjustable Wrench · How to Use a Level · How to Calculate Square Footage · How to Turn Off a Toilet Water Line · How to Unclog a Toilet · How to Clear a Clogged Sink Drain · How to Check the Circuit Breakers · How to Find a Stud in the Wall · How to Hang a Picture · How to Fix a Small Hole in a Wall

Notes   297

Introduction

*H*ere's a question every girl wants the answer to: *When exactly does a girl become a woman?* If you are thinking the correct answer has something to do with age, cultural rites of passage, or changes in a girl's body, then you are on the right track.

Around the world, cultures celebrate the transition from girlhood to womanhood in unique and significant ways. Some wait for a specific age to mark the moment officially. In the US, adulthood is legally recognized on your 18th birthday. Yet in the UK, 16 is the magic number. In Japan and New Zealand you'll need to turn 20, and if you live in Zambia, waiting until you are 21 years old to be lawfully recognized as an adult may feel like an eternity.

Cultural traditions also play an important part in a girl's "coming of age." In many regions of Central and South America, girls celebrate their quinceañera at 15 by renewing their baptismal vows in a Catholic mass and hosting a fiesta for friends and family. In Japan, some girls still celebrate a 1,200-year-old tradition known as Seijin no Hi, recognizing a youth's age of maturity by dressing up in their finest traditional attire and celebrating with friends and family who shower them with gifts. In Malaysia, some Muslim girls consider their 11th birthday to be very special as it marks the time when they can celebrate Khatam Al Koran. In the southwestern US, some traditional Apache girls still complete the Na'ii'ees Sunrise Ceremony, also known as the coming-of-age or the puberty ceremony, in which female participants draw closer to the first woman, Esdzanadehe.

Some mothers wait with great anticipation for their daughters to have their first menstruation and then throw them an elaborate "period party."

Also known as *lady's days*, the arrival of *Aunt Flo*, and *her time of the month*, the reality is the onset of a girl's menstrual cycle indicates her body is quickly changing, and some moms feel that's worth celebrating.

Truth be told, it's difficult to mark the exact moment a girl becomes a woman. Perhaps the answer to the question includes more than her age, traditions, or physical body. Here is what I can tell you with certainty: Strong women know that personal maturity transforms them into women. Maturity is a practiced skill and is best demonstrated when a woman knows how to do the right thing, the right way, at the right time, for the right reason.

So, will knowing how to do stuff and behave "properly" actually make you a woman? Nope! Growing up takes time, practice, and some difficult trials. As you navigate the journey to womanhood, learn and grow not just your skills, but also your character. Character? Yes, *character* is who you are and what you do . . . even when nobody's watching. It's repeated patterns, decisions you make, and actions you take that develop the picture of who you are and who you will become. Strong women live by different standards—higher standards. Strong women don't believe that the type of clothes they wear, how much they spend, or the number of shoes they own are what makes them a woman. Strong women know that maturity, character, and being kind to themselves and others helps define them.

Give yourself the knowledge and tools to become a strong, confident, and capable woman too. This *Girls' Guide to Conquering Life* is packed full of real-life, useful how-to instructions that will make your journey to womanhood a little smoother. It's loaded with quotes, fun facts, and wisdom from women who are experts in their field—women who can fix stuff, can demonstrate good character, and can handle social situations with grace and confidence.

Now it's your turn!

I'm *strong* because I'm fearless.

I'm *fearless* because I'm confident.

I'm *confident* because I am
capable of doing what is required
of me and what inspires me.

My *knowledge*, my *talents*,
my *strengths* are all practiced,
and practice makes me better.

Better at being *myself*,
better at being *kind* to all,
and better at *helping* others
become *strong* too.

1

Guys & Dating

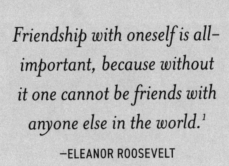

Friendship with oneself is all–important, because without it one cannot be friends with anyone else in the world.[1]

—ELEANOR ROOSEVELT

*Y*ou may find them to be overly annoying. You may catch yourself staring at them way too much. Loathe them or like them, guys make up about half of the earth's population, so there's no avoiding them. One thing is certain—before you consider who is "datable" or not, take the time to get to know the one person who will be in all your relationships: yourself.

Getting to know yourself is a lifelong adventure. Just a few years ago, you were a little girl with a little girl's thoughts and a little girl's body. In a few years you'll be a grown woman who thinks and looks much different. But now you're at the age when almost everything is changing, and changing fast. What you like to do is changing. Some of the people you like are changing. Who you want to become may be changing too. This is totally normal and an important part of the adventure and transformation between girlhood and womanhood. The truth is, the more you discover what matters most to you, the more you will enjoy the journey. To help you focus on the true you, complete these statements with confidence before starting any dating relationship.

- My goals are . . .
- My priorities are . . .
- My beliefs and values are . . .

You are 100% you and only 50% of any relationship, so knowing and owning these statements will help you be confident in yourself before somebody else enters the picture. Knowing your priorities will keep your vision clear; say yes to what is important and no to what is not. Staying true to your beliefs balances your heart, mind, body, and soul. This all adds up to you growing into a woman who does not limit or sacrifice herself for the sake of any relationship.

If you are confident in who you are, you'll be better prepared when "datable" does come along. Your standards are high, so his better be too. If you are going to become a 50/50 couple, you'll need to respect each other's goals, priorities, beliefs, and values. If that isn't happening . . . neither is the relationship.

When you meet someone who honors you fully, you've found someone special. As in any relationship, communication is important and can make or break you as a couple. Communication is not just talk, talk, talking—it's also about truly listening to understand. What is communicated through tone of voice, eye contact, and body language also says a lot. Working on your communication skills is important at any stage of a relationship. Here are a few pointers about good communication:

1. **Say what you mean to say.** Work on your ability to use words properly, keeping in mind the tone and volume of your voice. Speech can be an amazing, powerful tool. It helps to have a good vocabulary, so pay closer attention in English class. It's been said that words can cut deep, so choose them wisely, especially if you like sarcasm. Too much or mistimed sarcasm can cause both you and others unintended pain. Remember, sometimes saying less is more. Like when a simple "yes" means "yes" and "no" means "no," you'll need to stand behind your words.

2. **Know your body language.** How you physically hold yourself while speaking provides clues to what you are feeling and thinking. For instance, slouch your shoulders and look down and you'll appear to lack confidence or maybe even look weak. Cross your arms and tap your foot and you look upset or impatient. Instead, stand tall and look people in the eyes when they talk. This tells them you are listening and interested in what they have to say.

3. **Listen to understand.** There is a big difference between hearing and listening. Hearing is easy, but listening to understand takes practice. You hear the words coming out of someone's mouth, but do you really understand what they are saying? Try paying attention to their body language and repeating a variation of what they said to confirm you understood what they meant. You're not "judging" their words, just affirming their intent and confirming you understand them correctly.

Do keep this not-so-fun fact in mind: More often than not, dating relationships end with a breakup. Yes, it's true, "datable" might prove to be less than remarkable. This is just one reason why good communication is so important. Go slow when you decide to start dating. Rushing into a relationship emotionally or physically rarely ends well. Building a relationship on the quality of your friendship makes the potential breakup statement "let's just be friends" less likely to actually happen.

Talk with a Guy You Like

YOU WILL NEED:
- A guy you like
- Courage
- Fresh breath

TIME REQUIRED:
As long as it takes

*T*his is no big deal. Then again, sometimes it feels like it's the biggest deal in the world, right?! Talking to someone you like can make you more nervous than anything else imaginable. Just keep in mind, this kind of nervous is another way of knowing you are excited to talk with him. So, be confident and know you got this! Just go up to him and say something simple like "Hello" followed by a conversation-starting statement or open-ended question that gets him talking.

Breathe. Taking a couple deep breaths is a good idea anytime you need to relax, so take some now! The extra oxygen will help keep you calm, cool, and confident.

Check your breath. This is a first-impression thing—no need to leave him with an impression of the last meal you ate. Do a double check and maybe eat a mint to freshen up your introduction. (See "How to Freshen Bad Breath.")

Approach with confidence. Stand tall with your shoulders back and your head held high.

Say something. Maybe start with a simple, "Hello, I'm [your name here]." It's best to be yourself, so if you prefer a "Howdy," "What's up," or "Hey," that's your call.

Ask open-ended questions. If you would like to spend more than ten seconds talking with someone, asking a few good questions is a good way to get a conversation going. A few yes/no questions will work if you don't know them very well, but open-ended questions that require explanations are the best! If you ask the questions, make sure you are a good listener and that you are ready to answer if questions are asked of you.

You may need to think of a few open-ended questions before you say "hello" (or whatever). Here are some examples:

- ▶ "What kind of music do you like?" and "Have you ever seen them in concert?"
- ▶ "What's your favorite class?" and "Why do you like that class so much?"
- ▶ "Watched any good movies lately?" and "Would you recommend I see it too?"

End the conversation well. Wrap things up with a positive statement like, "Good talking with you. See you again soon." There's nothing wrong with simple!

Did You Know?

Girls use their "sophisticated verbal talents" to bond in relationships. When engaging in meaningful discussions, girls often maintain eye contact, lean in, and enjoy lots of talking. This helps cement the bond they have with each other. This is rarely the case with boys.[2]

Invite a Guy on a First Date

YOU WILL NEED:
- A guy you want to ask on a date
- Confidence
- Fresh breath (see "How to Freshen Bad Breath")

TIME REQUIRED:
It may seem longer than it actually takes.

*P*repare yourself. What you are about to attempt may end up ranking in the top 10 most memorable moments of your life. The first-date-invite story could be told for years to come and from two perspectives—yours and his. How you plan and undertake the asking determines if the story told will be epic or horrific.

Choose carefully. A date is about getting to know somebody better. Dating will help you learn what type of guy you are interested in and what type of guy is interested in you.

Pick an event. He is more likely to say yes to a date if you have a specific event in mind. Think of something fun that he would be interested in doing too.

Plan your transportation. Avoid long rides, as they are not usually first-date friendly.

Plan your ask. Give him at least two or three days between asking and when you plan on going out. If you want the date to be on Friday, ask him on Tuesday or Wednesday. He may need to ask his parents, arrange a ride, and maybe earn some money. And anticipation is half the fun of a good first date. (And before talking with him, see "How to Freshen Bad Breath.")

Ask him out. Timing and approach is everything. With confidence, describe your plans and ask if he would like to join you. And remember, asking in person is always best!

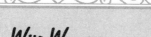

Wise Woman

There is no guarantee he will say yes to a date with you. What is guaranteed is if you never ask, he will never say yes.

Plan a Date

YOU WILL NEED:		TIME REQUIRED:
• A guy who said yes to a date with you • Confidence	• Pen and paper • Money • Transportation	1 hour of planning

*I*f you want a date to go great, you will need to put some thought and energy in before you two go out. The best way to ensure he brags to his buddies about your great date is to dedicate some T.I.M.E. to pre-planning and preparing. Here's how.

STEP 1

Think it. Try to think about the date from both your perspectives. What would he like to do too? What do you have in common?

Date To-Do's
1) Dinner reservation
2) Movie times
3) Transportation
4) Budget: $35
5) Pick-up/Drop-off times

Ink it. Write down your date ideas on a piece of paper. Brainstorming is a creative way to test an idea, see potential conflicts, and identify your best options. Consider costs, transportation, timing, and perhaps even getting the "okay" from both your parents.

Map it. Once you have your best idea written down, map out your plan.

- When is the date? Day, evening, night?
- When does the date begin? He needs a specific time.
- What is your budget? A date can get expensive, so set a budget and stick to it.
- Who is paying? Going "dutch" is good if you want to keep things simple. (See "How to Decide Who Pays on a Date.")
- Where are you going? Be specific. For example, plan for dinner at a specific location vs. finding a place.
- How will you get there? Will you meet him there? Will you pick him up, or will he pick you up? Will you be driving?
- When does the date end? If you're the one driving, have him home on time. Be specific and honor your commitment. This is one way you will gain the favor and trust of his parents.

Enjoy it. Have a fun date. Hopefully he will appreciate the effort.

Did You Know?

Many states have laws for new drivers restricting unrelated passengers and driving during certain hours. If you will be driving, know the laws before a police officer explains them to you—in front of your date.

Decide Who Pays on a Date

YOU WILL NEED:
- A planned date
- Money

TIME REQUIRED:
1-minute conversation

*D*ating etiquette established over a century ago has become ancient history. Back in the day, the guy paid for everything on a date. Today's modern woman often wants to pay for some or even all of a date. So who picks up the tab? She? He? We? Here is a simple and respectful way to decide who opens their purse/wallet without opening yourselves up to controversy.

Who asked who? Often, whoever did the inviting and planning of the date is the one who pays (unless it's talked about during the invite). Still, don't assume. It's a good idea to talk about it so there are no surprises when the bill comes. If you are doing the inviting, let him know up front if you will cover the date cost or if you want to split the bill.

STEP **2**

Dates #3 and beyond. Sounds like you may be on your way to having an official boyfriend. If you are not sure yet, wait a few more dates, then think about having the DTR (Define The Relationship) talk. Once you have determined that, yep, he's your boyfriend, keep the money-spending lines of communication open. The word *boyfriend* is a compound word uniting "boy" with "friend." True friends complement each other in all areas, including money. Talk about it and work together to spend and pay appropriately while dating.

Fact or Fiction:

I can't afford to date.

Fiction. The fact is, you can't put a price on love, but you can on a date. You don't have to spend big CA$H to show a guy you're creative, considerate, and worth going on date #2 with next week. Dates should be fun, not defunding.

Meet a Guy's Parents for the First Time

YOU WILL NEED:	TIME REQUIRED:
• Confident handshake • Smile • Manners	1–5 minutes

Meeting the parents of the guy you like can be scary if you don't already know them. This is an official first-impression situation, and first impressions have a tendency to stick around in our memories. You want to make sure it's a good impression in the hopes they will be more likely to be happy with you spending time with their son.

Make eye contact. When greeting his parents, look them in the eyes. Comfortable eye contact is 4–5 seconds, pause by briefly looking away (to avoid staring), and then make eye contact again.

Smile. An authentic smile conveys optimism and high levels of confidence.

Speak with confidence. Start by saying something simple yet polite, like, "Nice to meet you, Mrs. [last name] and Mr. [last name]."

Shake hands. Follow the "How to Shake Hands" steps. By extending a friendly and traditional greeting, you show them you are respectful and know how to interact with adults.

Be yourself. Don't put on a show.

Use your manners. Say "please" and "thank you," "yes" rather than "yeah," "no" rather than "nah," and "excuse me?" rather than "huh?" Chew with your mouth closed, don't talk about yourself too much, and by all means, control any socially awkward bodily functions.

Helpful Hint

Moms look out for their sons' best interests. If you are interested in her son and her son is interested in you, you need to be looking out for his best interests too. When you do this and understand what the son's mom cares about, she will possibly consider *you* to be in her son's best interest, and you'll be able to spend more time with him without scorn from his mama.

Balance Time
with Boyfriend vs. Girlfriends

YOU WILL NEED:
· Friends
· Boyfriend

TIME REQUIRED:
Daily life

*G*ood relationships take time. Spending too much time with your "boo" can be frustrating for your BFFs and even cause friendship failure. Take care not to tip the time balance so far that your friends start to feel like you abandoned them for him. The truth is, many dating relationships don't last long, and your boo may soon be a ghost—while your truest girlfriends might be around for a lifetime!

Don't smother each other. The fastest way to drive a guy away is to take up all his free time. There is truth in the old saying, "Absence makes the heart grow fonder." Even if you have the same group of friends, it's good to spend some time apart.

Plan time together. Once a week take the time to plan a date, just the two of you. A date doesn't have to be grand or expensive. Think fun. (See "How to Plan a Date.")

Mix it up. You should be able to hang out with both your BFFs and your boyfriend at the same time. Equally sharing time within a group of friends is a sign of maturity.

Fact or Fiction:
BFFs before BFs.

Fact, if you are planning on living with your best friend forever. That is until your BFF and their BF becomes BFFs and they choose each other over you.

Fiction. The truth is, best friend are good both now and in the future, yet one day you and someone very special may choose to get married and put each other first, over all others.

Respectfully Break Up with a Guy

YOU WILL NEED:	TIME REQUIRED:
· Empathy · Quiet, semi-private or private location	5–30 minutes

If you choose to date, a breakup is probably going to occur at some point. Maybe the guy you're dating now is proving not to be the one for you, and to keep the relationship going would be unfair. When this happens, be true to yourself and let the relationship go. Remember, breaking up doesn't have to be a big, dramatic, ugly thing. Keep your emotions calm and avoid saying things that will make the situation worse. Keep your words respectful and think of how you would feel if the same break-up words you say to him were said to you.

STEP **1**

Consider your words. Know what you are going to say before you speak. Practice if you need to.

STEP **2**

Pick the place. If possible, decide where you will talk in person, face-to-face, in a private enough space that embarrassment over possible tears can be avoided. Never break up via a text message or on social media.

IMPORTANT

If you ever feel that a breakup could become violent or emotionally harmful, seek help first.

STEP **3**

Respect his feelings. He may respond with sadness, surprise, frustration, or he may even get mad and try to blame you. The only person you can control is you, so keep calm and confident in your decision.

STEP **4**

Keep it positive. Following your breakup, only speak of the good aspects of your relationship. Hopefully you two shared some good times, so honor those memories and talk publicly only about the positive. If you don't have anything positive to say, don't say anything at all.

IMPORTANT

If you have been mistreated in any way, seek help from an adult you trust.

Did You Know?

Neil Sedaka's 1962 song "Breaking Up Is Hard to Do" hit #1 on the *Billboard* Hot 100. Since its debut last century, the heartbreak song has been rerecorded by more than 32 professional artists. It just goes to show that time doesn't change the fact that breaking up is hard to do.

2

Social Skills & Manners

Manners are a sensitive awareness of the feelings of others. If you have that awareness, you have good manners, no matter what fork you use.[1]

—EMILY POST

*M*anners and social skills are very cultural. In the US we have diverse cultures with different social customs and unique protocols for proper interaction. In spite of that diversity, there are some settings in which etiquette unique to American culture is expected. For example, here's a personal experience I (Erica) had in high school.

I had been invited to dinner for the first time at my boyfriend's house. We ate with his parents in their dining room with all the formal settings of a "proper" American table. As we ate dinner, I noticed my boyfriend staring at me—and it wasn't in an adoring kind of way. Then he asked, "Why are you eating like that?"

I was a bit shocked and very embarrassed. I thought I had good table manners. I was NOT eating with my mouth open. I had my napkin in my lap. My elbows weren't on the table. Yet something about the way I was eating was freaking him out. Thankfully his mother spoke up and said to her son, "Well, that was rude!" She then turned to me and asked, "Isn't your family from Europe?" I replied, "Yes, the Netherlands." Turning back to her son she said, "Jonathan, that is the way people eat in the Netherlands. Leave her alone."

We then had a fun discussion about the different ways cultures gather and enjoy meals together. Up to that night I hadn't known it wasn't appropriate in formal settings in America to use the knife to push food onto the fork. Not setting down the knife between bites was totally normal in my family. But not with my boyfriend's. What I learned in that dinner conversation was a good lesson in formal table manners, American style, which has helped me in other formal meals throughout the years. What my then-boyfriend/now-husband learned was not to ask such rude questions in front of others. LOL!

Shake Hands

YOU WILL NEED:	TIME REQUIRED:
· Clean hands	3 seconds
· Authentic smile	
· Confidence	

Shaking hands is an important part of making a good first impression. The palm-pressing tradition started back in medieval times as a way of showing that neither greeter held a concealed weapon. The tradition holds true today for those who grasp the significance of trust, respect, and honor. Mastering the handshake is one way to show new acquaintances, teachers, co-workers, bosses, and your boyfriend's parents that you are friendly, confident, and respectful.

Make eye contact. With an authentic smile on your face, look the person in the eyes as you prepare to shake their hand. Just don't lock on with a creepy, wide-eyed stare.

STEP **2**

Prepare to shake. Extend your right arm and hand toward the other person. With your hand open and your thumb pointing upward, direct your handshake to align with the center of your body.

STEP **3**

Meet in the middle. Keeping your extended arm slightly bent at the elbow, meet the other person's hand in the space half the distance between your body and theirs. The flat of your palm should meet theirs with fingers extended and thumb raised.

STEP **4**

Grasp hands. Use slight pressure to give their hand a firm but gentle squeeze. No limp-fish, wimpy handshakes allowed! (Hint: Pretend their hand is a small bird that needs to be held firmly enough to not fly away but not so tight it is crushed.)

STEP **5**

Shake hands. With your wrist locked, raise your hand upward about two inches and downward about two inches. One or two upward and downward shakes should be sufficient.

STEP **6**

Release hands. Simultaneously let go and lower your hand back to your side. Do not wipe your hand on your pants, even if their palm was sweaty.

More Info

In many cultures, making eye contact is a sign of interest and respect. In others, looking into the eyes is a sign of disrespect and even lust. Know what the traditions are where you are. As the saying goes, "When in Rome, do as the Romans do." *(Just an FYI: When shaking hands in Rome, be sure to maintain eye contact while greeting people. Otherwise, Italians may think you are hiding something.)*

Introduce Yourself

YOU WILL NEED:
- Confident handshake
- Friendly smile

TIME REQUIRED:
30 seconds

Sometimes you just have to put yourself out there. Instead of waiting for people to introduce themselves to you, be proactive and make the introduction yourself. Your confident personal introduction communicates openness when meeting new people and interest in expanding your real-world social network.

STEP **1**

Approach with confidence. Keep your shoulders back and head up when approaching the person you want to meet.

Smile. A friendly smile makes for a great first impression.

Make eye contact. Look them in the eyes, yet don't lock in too strong with a creepy stare.

Meet and greet. Just prior to offering a friendly handshake, meet the other person with a greeting that includes your name, possible connection, and reason for your introducing yourself.

EXAMPLE:

"Hello. I'd like to introduce myself. My name is Amy and I believe you work with my mom. She tells me you attended the same university I am considering. May I ask you a few questions about why you chose that school and your experience there?"

Shake hands. Extending a confident handshake is both a respectful and professional way of showing you are an open and friendly person. (See "How to Shake Hands.")

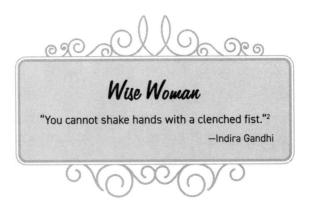

Wise Woman

"You cannot shake hands with a clenched fist."[2]

—Indira Gandhi

Introduce Other People

YOU WILL NEED:

- Two or more people needing an introduction
- Their full names locked in your memory
- Some positive information to share about each person

TIME REQUIRED:

2 minutes

*P*roperly introducing two or more people is an important skill to learn. When people you know also know each other, you gain a reputation as a connector. Connectors keep introductions comfortable and never create a situation that obligates people to start a friendship. If they hit it off, that's great. Thanks for the introduction!

Show respect. Either start with the person you've known the longest and then the others based on connection with that person, or start by introducing the most senior person in the group then work your way to the youngest.

Use full names. Whenever possible, introduce people using both their first and last name.

EXAMPLE:

"Coach, I'd like to introduce you to my mom, Erica Catherman." Next, turning the introduction to Coach: "Mom, this is my coach, Clara Jones."

Share something personal. People want to know and be known, so say something positive and personal about the people you are introducing to demonstrate that you value them.

EXAMPLE:

Starting with Mom: "Coach, my mom was on the rowing team at her university." Now turn the focus to your coach: "Mom, Coach Jones was on the soccer team at her university."

Restate names. By stating and restating people's names in your introduction, you help others better remember the people they are meeting.

Set up the win-win. Always try to show a good reason why the people you are introducing could find value in knowing each other.

EXAMPLE:

"Coach Jones, I remember you telling us to focus on keeping our grades up the second half of the season. Well, my mom is an engineer and is pretty good at helping me with my math homework. She is willing to tutor our team twice a week if that would help some of our players raise their math grades."

Step back. Now that the personal introductions are done, let people talk. You set them up with names, personal information, and a win-win opportunity. Now let them take the next steps.

Fact or Fiction:

Sticking your tongue out can be polite.

Fact. When in Tibet, it is good manners to poke your tongue out when being introduced. The tradition dates back to the ninth century when a cruel Tibetan king named Lang Darma was discovered to have a black tongue. People hated the king and feared meeting his reincarnation. Following his death they started sticking out their tongues when greeting to prove they weren't the king, version 2.0.

Listen Well

YOU WILL NEED:	TIME REQUIRED:
· Undivided attention	As long as it takes
· Pure intentions	
· Conversation place	

Some say listening is an art that utilizes the ears, eyes, mind, and heart. Others believe listening is a skill developed over time through self-discipline and hard work. The truth is, listening well is both a beautiful art and a practiced skill.

Face-to-face with family, out with friends, while at work, or in public, most people simply want to be heard and understood. Listening well is about focusing your attention on others with the intent to understand them

first. This doesn't mean you have to agree with them, take their side, or change your mind. Listening well is about you tuning out distractions and tuning in your focus on what somebody else is saying to hear more than their words, to discover more in their meaning.

STEP 1

Put away distractions. Give the other person your undivided attention by putting away your phone, tablet, computer, or any other distraction.

STEP 2

Focus your attention. By turning your focus toward the other person, you demonstrate that they have your undivided attention. Face your body toward them, make good eye contact, and if you are seated, lean slightly forward.

STEP 3

Listen closely. Hear the words they are saying. Pay special attention to the tone, volume, and pace of their voice. Their body language may also communicate a variety of emotions like excitement, frustration, or concern.

STEP 4

Ask questions. Asking questions can keep the conversation moving. The trick is to know the right kind of questions to ask. Here are four guidelines to asking questions:

- Stay on topic.
- Ask open-ended questions that require more than a yes or no answer.
- Never ask, "Want to know what I think?" or "You know what I'd do if I were you?"
- Don't judge.

STEP 5

Nod your head. Knowingly or not, people pick up on nonverbal communication. By nodding your head, you let them know you are trying to understand what they are saying.

Repeat to confirm. Give the other person the confidence you are understanding them by briefly recapping what they have shared with you. Try not to parrot back their exact words. Do capture a combination of what they said and how they are feeling as you repeat to confirm what they have shared.

Did You Know?

How we communicate is so much more than the words we choose. Communication is a combination of these elements:

7% words—choose your words carefully and stay away from extreme descriptions like "always" or "never," "everybody" and "nobody";

38% tone of voice—speak up so they can hear you, talk clearly, and be respectful—no sarcasm; and

55% body language—face people when you talk, look them in the eye, and smile.

Speak Up for Yourself or Others

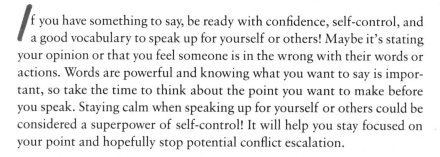

YOU WILL NEED:
- Confidence
- Self-control

TIME REQUIRED:
As long as it takes

If you have something to say, be ready with confidence, self-control, and a good vocabulary to speak up for yourself or others! Maybe it's stating your opinion or that you feel someone is in the wrong with their words or actions. Words are powerful and knowing what you want to say is important, so take the time to think about the point you want to make before you speak. Staying calm when speaking up for yourself or others could be considered a superpower of self-control! It will help you stay focused on your point and hopefully stop potential conflict escalation.

Know what you want to say and identify your main point. Choose your words carefully and stay focused on the issue and keeping to your point. Going off topic will make your point unclear.

Be direct and confident. There is no need to speak around the issue. Be direct and confident while making eye contact and speaking clearly, and focus on maintaining a calm, controlled voice tone and volume. Avoid accusations, cursing, and anything said in hate.

Find a conclusion or resolution. Once you have made your point, look for next steps. The issue may be resolved or you may need to keep moving toward a positive outcome. If possible, work together with the people in the conflict to find a solution. If you can't reach consensus, find support from someone you trust (such as a teacher or mentor) so you can continue to stand up for yourself or others affected by the situation.

Did You Know?

The tone of your voice changes as the volume of speaking increases. The louder you speak the higher pitch your voice becomes. To maintain a controlled and smooth tone of voice, keep the volume level normal, controlled, and consistent.

Open the Door for Another Person

YOU WILL NEED:
• Hinged door

TIME REQUIRED:
5 seconds

Whether you are being polite or just passing through too, knowing how to open the door for another person is a good way to show both respect and consideration for friends and strangers alike. It can also help make someone's day by showing a bit of goodwill. Such an act of kindness will be appreciated by family and your boss, and can figuratively help "open doors" for you in the future. Getting it right all hinges on knowing why, when, and how to push, pull, or step through.

Know why and when. Why? Because you are a considerate, respect-ful, patient, thoughtful, humble, and all-around nice girl who treats others like she wants to be treated. When? Whenever your sister, mom, grandma, and friends are going through the same door as you. For your boss, co-workers, and customers. For your coach, teachers, principal, substitute, janitor, and especially the lunch lady. Basically, open the door for anybody you have an opportunity to serve.

Identify which way the door opens. Right or left, in or out? Look at the handle and hinges: For example, if the hinges are visible and the handle is on the right, the door swings toward you and to the left. If the handle is on the left, it swings right. No visible hinges means you will push to open.

Arrive early. You need to arrive a step or two before the other person. Avoid reaching around them to open the door. This crowds the space and forces the other person to awkwardly step away from you.

Open the door. When you pull open a door, allow the other person to walk through first and then follow. When you push, walk through first and hold it open until the other person has passed and is safely clear of the door.

Don't leave them waiting. You are not obligated to hold the door for every person behind you. Holding it open for a few people is nice, yet being the doorman for a line of strangers is usually a paid position. And it's rude to leave the person with you waiting on the other side. So let the door close when there are a few steps between you and the next person headed for the door.

Did You Know?

Automatic door openers have been around for more than 2,000 years. The Greek scholar Heron of Alexandria, also known as . . . wait for it . . . "Hero," was a mathematician, engineer, and author credited with inventing the earliest known automatic door opener. Brilliantly built with a series of hydraulically driven weights, ropes, and pulleys, the automatic system opened the city gates and temple doors just as the people were arriving first thing in the day.

Set a Table

YOU WILL NEED:
· Plates   · Glasses
· Silverware   · Napkins

TIME REQUIRED:
30 seconds per setting

*G*et set to sit down. While delivery is fun for sofa-surfing gamers and binge movie watchers alike, other meals taste best when eaten at the table. By setting the table, you provide a casual way to invite family and friends to sit down and savor the flavor of time spent together over some good food.

STEP 1

Place the dinner plate. Set the dinner plate about one inch in from the table's edge, directly in front of where the person will be seated.

STEP 2

Place the side plate. If salad or bread will be served, place the smaller side plate to the upper left of the dinner plate.

STEP 3

Set the forks. Forks are set one inch to the left of the plate. The dinner fork is placed closest to the plate and smaller salad fork to the left of the dinner fork.

STEP 4

Set the knife. Knives are set one inch to the right of the plate. Position the cutting edge toward the plate.

STEP 5

Set the spoon. Spoons are set to the right of the knife.

STEP 6

Set the water glass. Water glasses are set to the upper right of the plate, above the knife.

STEP **7**

Set the napkin. Napkins are set to the left of the forks.

STEP **8**

Set another place. Space each additional place setting about 24 inches apart, if room allows.

Wise Woman

CHEW WITH YOUR MOUTH CLOSED! Neither I nor anyone else wants to see, re-see, and re-re-see your food as you grind it between your teeth. Close those lips while you chew. This will also restrict your ability to talk with your mouth full—which is also pretty gross!

Order from a Menu

YOU WILL NEED:
• Restaurant
• Menu

TIME REQUIRED:
3 minutes

There is more to ordering than selecting a number or slogan-titled meal option. Any girl can pick a #3 meal deal from a wall-mounted picture-perfect "menu." It's time to grow up, sit down, spread a napkin on your lap, and order from a menu held in your hands. It's true: Menu dining requires more time and preparation. The good thing is, so does the meal you will enjoy. Add to the experience ambiance, friends, and three courses of food you can savor, and you may discover ordering from a menu is your new #1 favorite way to eat out.

STEP 1

Order drinks. Your first consideration will be beverages. If water is desired, order it now, as some restaurants will not serve it unless requested. Your server usually will take your drink order first to give you some time to consider the menu options.

STEP 2

Review the menu. Look the entire menu over. The first listings are usually starters or appetizers. Next come entrées or main courses and side dishes. Desserts are offered toward the end of the menu. Try to narrow down your choices before the server returns for your food order.

STEP 3

Pair appetizers. If an appetizer looks good, ask those dining with you if they too would enjoy anything pre-meal. Pair your selection with the tastes of all who wish to share.

STEP **4**

Ask about specials. Ask your server for today's specials. After the dish descriptions have been given, ask for the price of any specials you find appetizing. Remember, specials can be more expensive than the menu's daily entrées.

STEP **5**

Order entrées. Tell your server what your entrée selection will be for dinner. Be sure to have read and selected which side dishes come with your meal. If a salad is included in your selection, choose what type of dressing you would like served.

STEP **6**

Consider dessert. Once your meal is complete, consider ordering dessert. In most restaurants it is acceptable to share a single serving of dessert between two people.

Fact or Fiction:

Restaurant menus can make you sick.

Fact. You may read a restaurant menu and think, "Yuck! That lamb stew special looks sickening." But have you ever considered that the menu you are holding could actually make you puke? Few restaurants clean their menus between customers. That means other diners' dirty hands held that same menu you are holding now. You follow them, touch your food, and put that food in your mouth. Holding a menu can't be avoided, but keeping it from touching your plate or silverware can be done. That and seriously consider washing your hands after ordering.

Leave a Tip

YOU WILL NEED:	TIME REQUIRED:
• Good service • Money	30 seconds

*T*he practice of offering gratuity has been part of the American hospitality industry for a few hundred years. Gratuity is also called a *tip*: think of the acronym "to insure promptitude." A few hundred years ago, a tip was given before service to ensure faster and better care was given to those who tipped over those who didn't. Today a tip is given after service in appreciation for prompt attention and good service.

STEP **1**

Assess the service. Consider the quality of the service you were provided. Was it below, average, or above the standard you expected?

Do the math. If the average tip for average service is 20% of the pre-tax bill, this means that when your pre-tax bill is $25.00, the tip is $5.00. And if you use a discount coupon, your tip should be based on the full amount before tax.

Below average = 10% to 15%
Average = 18% to 20%
Above average = More than 20%

Leave the tip. When you pay, add the tip to your final bill. If you are paying with cash, leave the cash tip sitting on the table.

More Info

Heads up! Some restaurants automatically add gratuity, or a "service fee," to the bill when your dining group is five or more people. So be sure to check the bottom of your bill to see if gratuity has already been added or not.
Who gets gratuity?

Service staff, Hair stylist = 15% to 20% of pre-tax bill
Valet parking attendant = $1.00 to $3.00
Coatroom attendant = $1.00 per coat
Restroom attendant = $1.00
Delivery driver = 15%
Café tip jar = 5% to 10%

Wrap a Gift

YOU WILL NEED:		TIME REQUIRED:
· Gift	· Tape	5 minutes
· Box for gift	· Scissors	
· Event-appropriate	· Ribbon or peel-	
wrapping paper	and-stick bow	
· Packing material,		
if needed		

*W*ell, it's the thought that counts" is an excuse joke for a poorly wrapped gift. Um . . . no! Presentation is important. A well-wrapped present will be admired and complimented prior to the paper-peeling. Wrap a gift just right, and the receiver may even save the perfect paper as a memento of your thoughtfulness or decide to reuse such nice paper. With a few quick tips and a little practice, you too can elevate your wrapping from wasteful to wow!

STEP 1

Gather your materials. On a flat surface, gather your gift, box, wrapping paper, tape, ribbon, and scissors.

STEP 2

Box the gift. Place the gift in a like-sized box. If the item is fragile, be sure to cushion it inside the box with packing material like tissue paper or bubble wrap.

STEP 3

Measure wrapping paper. Unroll the wrapping paper to measure a few inches longer than the distance around the box.

STEP 4

Cut wrapping paper. Use scissors to cut the wrapping paper free from the roll. Cut as straight as you can.

STEP 5

Trim wrapping paper. Cut the sides of the paper so they will fold up a little less than the height of the box's ends.

STEP 6

Wrap four sides. Place the gift box upside down in the center of the wrapping paper. Bring one long end of the paper up and over the box. Secure the end of the paper with tape just past the center of the bottom of the box. Repeat on the other side with the addition of folding over the very end of the paper to hide the cut edge.

STEP 7

Wrap one end. Pick one of the two open ends and fold the paper down to meet the side of the box. This will create two paper triangles on either side. Fold the triangles in and secure them with tape. Now bring up the remaining flap of paper, fold over the end, and tape.

STEP 8

Wrap remaining end. Repeat STEP 7 on the other end of the box.

Add bow or ribbon. Finish off the gift-wrapping with a decorative peel-and-stick bow or, if you're up to the challenge, first wrap it neatly with a ribbon and then complete it with a handmade bow.

Did You Know?

Before Hallmark invented wrapping paper in 1917, brown paper or tissue paper were the most common items used to wrap gifts. Today, 2.6 billion dollars is spent on wrapping paper each year.

Clean a Bathroom

YOU WILL NEED:

- Rubber gloves
- Shower cleaner
- Window cleaner
- Toilet bowl cleaner
- Disinfectant cleaner
- Toilet bowl brush
- Microfiber cloths, paper towels, or newspaper
- Broom & dust pan
- Floor cleaner
- Mop & bucket

TIME REQUIRED:

15–30 minutes

*Y*our house may be your castle, but the cleanliness of your porcelain throne is the true expression of your reign. How you clean and keep your bathroom will either impress or disgust your guests. They may or may not look in your medicine cabinet for clues about your personal life, but they

are guaranteed to see the ring in the toilet and dried toothpaste splatter on the mirror. Cleaning your bathroom is not only healthy, it's a good way to keep your housekeeping reputation out of the toilet.

STEP **1**

Tidy the bathroom. Remove everything that does not belong in the bathroom and return it to its proper place.

STEP **2**

Scrub the shower and bathtub. Remove everything from the shower and spray it with shower cleaner. Scrub the walls and the basin in a circular motion from top to bottom. Spray the entire area with water to rinse off the cleaner, and wipe it down again with a damp cloth. Be sure to clean your faucet and showerhead as well.

STEP **3**

Clean the toilet. Wearing rubber gloves, pour toilet bowl cleaner around the rim of the toilet. Use the toilet bowl brush to scrub around the whole inside of the toilet, including under the rim. Use the disinfectant cleaner to spray the entire outside of the toilet, including the handle, top of toilet, and under the toilet seat. Using a paper towel, wipe down every surface on your toilet. Take off your gloves before continuing to clean the rest of the bathroom.

STEP **4**

Shine the mirror. Using window cleaner, spray down your mirror and wipe it with a fresh microfiber cloth, paper towels, or newspaper.

STEP **5**

Wipe the countertops. Use a disinfectant cleaner to spray down the countertops, sink, fixtures, and faucets. Using a clean cloth or paper towel, wipe down all surfaces right away to prevent spotting or streaking.

STEP **6**

Clean the floors. Starting from the farthest corner of the room, sweep and then mop toward the door.

Take out the trash. Empty the trash and make sure that the inside and outside of the can is clean.

Did You Know?

Close the toilet lid before you flush. When the water rushes into the bowl, droplets of toilet water, urine, and feces become airborne. For this exact reason, put your toothbrush in a drawer or keep it as far away from the toilet as possible.

Make a Bed

YOU WILL NEED:

- Fitted bottom sheet
- Flat sheet
- Comforter
- Blanket (optional)
- Pillows
- Pillowcases

TIME REQUIRED:

1–3 minutes

Why should a girl make her bed when she's just going to get back in it later? After all, don't the experts recommend airing out the sheets each morning? They do, and you should. You should also take pride in the appearance of your room. You don't want your bed to look like a bad dream kept you thrashing about all night. It only takes a minute to make your bed and the result is way better than friends seeing your drool-stained pillow and faded My Little Pony sheets. Okay, maybe it's time for some new bedding!

Fit the bottom sheet. Take the fitted sheet and pull the elastic corners down and over each corner of the mattress.

STEP **2**

Spread the top sheet. The top of the flat sheet has a wide hem and should align even with the top of the bed, while the bottom of the sheet should hang off the foot of the bed.

STEP **3**

Tuck in the top sheet. At the foot of the bed, lift one mattress corner to tuck the bottom length of sheet into the space between the mattress and box spring. Repeat this process for the other corner.

STEP **4** (optional)

Spread your blanket. If you like additional layers of warmth on the bed, repeat STEP 3 with a light blanket.

STEP **5**

Spread the comforter. Make sure both sides and bottom of the comforter drape evenly over the bed.

STEP **6**

Place the pillows. Put the pillowcases on the pillows. Fluff the pillows and place them at the top of your bed.

More Info

It's a good practice to replace your pillow every year. The fact is that within 2 years of nightly use, one-third of your pillow's weight consists of dead skin and dust mites and their droppings. Nasty! So get a new pillow and you really will sleep tight—don't let the bedbugs bite.

3

Work & Ethics

The truth is, women can do anything they want. There is absolutely no limit on what we can achieve, and I hope that every young woman approaches life that way. We can become even more successful if we support each other, empower each other, and mentor the next generation so they can stand on our shoulders.[1]

—MICHELLE OBAMA, former First Lady

*Y*ou want to know a secret about work? The kind of secret few people know and even fewer people know what to do with? Of course you do—you're still reading, aren't you! Okay, here it is: *The big secret to work is . . . get a job you love and you'll never really "work" a day in your life.*

The best part about this secret is, it's true. Considering we spend a great deal of our lives at work, who wouldn't want to enjoy the 8 to 10 hours a day committed to the job? People who love their work are known for saying stuff like, "I can't believe I get paid to do this" and "I can't imagine doing anything else." They tend to take great pride in what they do and are quick to share with others how they too can gain greater satisfaction in a job well done. One woman who loves what she does and shares freely how to succeed in work and life is the executive director of the Ada Jenkins Families and Careers Development Center, Mrs. Georgia Kruger.

Spoiler alert: Georgia Kruger is a boss. Literally and figuratively. In addition to her job as a leader in promoting the importance of education and equal opportunity for all citizens, Georgia is a certified Pilates instructor, a seasoned road warrior, and fully devoted to her family. She is committed to excellence in all she does and is willing to share her secrets to success with anybody who's interested.

Georgia believes there are two primary values we all need to develop in order to succeed in work and life. "Authenticity and integrity are two of the most important qualities a person can possess. Authenticity means you are real. Far too often people aren't who they try to project or say they are. Integrity means you actually do what you say you are going to do. Let your yes be yes and your no be no. Which means if we have agreed on something, a handshake should be all that is needed."[2] What? A handshake is all that is needed in an agreement? That sounds dangerous. What if people change their minds later? "Sure, get it in writing, because contracts are a required part of business. But I would tell anybody, any day, that the most critical thing needed to both getting and keeping a job is your relationships." Georgia goes on to add, "You will not get the support you need if you do not nurture and maintain relationships. Relationships are a critical part of every single work equation. Relationships are built on trust. So, speak the truth, do what you say you'll do, and always do the right thing."

Georgia also sees the other side of some people in the workplace. The darker, not-so-honest, not-my-problem, it's-not-my-fault side. "When you make a mistake, take responsibility for your actions. Be willing to own your mistakes as opposed to trying to cover them up or make less of them. Unfortunately, that is something that happens often in the workplace. Which gets us back to the integrity issue." As a boss, Georgia understands that everyone makes mistakes. That's life. How people deal with their mistakes is what she believes reveals their true character. "People are always watching. Ask for it or not, you are a role model. How you conduct yourself at work—and everywhere, for that matter—sets an example for others to follow. So, take responsibility for your actions. If you make a mistake, accept it and do what you can to make it right."

In addition to authenticity and integrity, Georgia promotes the value of education to getting a good job. "Research shows a person who does not graduate from high school may never get a job that pays much above minimum wage. A person who graduates from high school is a little better off. The person who graduates from college is much better off." But what about the people not on the college track? Are they doomed to low wages for life? Not according to Georgia. "A trade school is also a very good thing. We are seeing the importance of a trade school education now more than ever. There are so many jobs—good-paying jobs—in the trades, and so few people are prepared to fill them."

To round out Georgia's advice about being the kind of applicant and employee bosses need, she recommends considering the company's culture. "I care less about your skillset than I do about who you are as a person. Will you fit in with the culture of our organization?" Georgia raises a good point, considering, for many people, the culture of a company is what makes or breaks their love for where they get to do their work.

Finally, life is not all about work, work, work. A healthy work-life balance is the secret to staying satisfied with both work and life. "Work is not the most important thing," Georgia cautions. "It's the fourth most important. Faith is first, family second, followed by friends, and then work." That doesn't mean you get to use the top three when you want an excuse to get out of work. "But we need a rhythm in life. That rhythm must include rest, and it must include margins. We can't let work pile up on, push aside, and overcome the other parts of our lives." To help set a work-life balance from the very beginning, Georgia recommends committing yourself to the kind of work that fits with your passions. "Think about the things that are life-giving to you. Professionally, the best kind of job for you will fuel your passions and dreams. Yes, you need to make a living, to make some money, but it's no big secret in life that you must be true to who you are and what you believe you can do."

Apply for a Job

YOU WILL NEED:

- A place you would like to work
- Job application and/or résumé and cover letter
- Telephone
- Computer or tablet with internet access

TIME REQUIRED:

Varies

STEP **1**

Contact the employer. On the company's website, check for available job openings. If the employer is a smaller company or is run by somebody you know, consider inquiring in person about any job openings. If there are opportunities available, clarify how to apply. Some employers require applications be submitted online, while others prefer you drop off the application in person. Be sure to write down the name of the hiring manager so future correspondence can be directed to the appropriate person.

Construct a résumé. If necessary, prepare a résumé and cover letter to include with the submission of your application.

STEP **3**

Fill out an application. If online, complete all required fields. If on paper, write clearly with a pen. (See "How to Fill Out an Application.")

> The big secret in life is that there is no big secret. Whatever your goal, you can get there if you're willing to work.[3]
>
> —OPRAH WINFREY

STEP **4**

Proofread. Be sure to edit and proofread your résumé, cover letter, and application prior to submission to ensure they are free of errors. This is critical in making a good impression on the hiring manager.

STEP **5**

Submit your application. If online, click submit. If on paper, turn in your completed application in person. DO NOT send your mother in as your messenger.

STEP **6**

Follow up. Several days after submitting your application, call the employer and ask to speak with the hiring manager. Confirm that your application was received and reviewed. Always be prepared to answer the hiring manager's questions and be willing to come in for an in-person interview.

Did You Know?

Posting your résumé online with a major job site is not going to be good enough. On average, about a half-million résumés are posted on top job sites each and every week. The best way to step to the front of the job opening line is to get in front of the employer, in person.

Fill Out an Application

YOU WILL NEED:

- Blank job application
- Black or blue ballpoint pen
- Professional and personal references
- At least one form of state or federal identification

TIME REQUIRED:

30–45 minutes

*A*pplications can be your potential employer's first impression of you. Make it a good impression by keeping the application neat, true, and complete. Make sure you use your best penmanship, answer all questions truthfully, and fill out all required information before turning in your application.

73

Target the market. You're going to put in some legwork to find a job, so before you do, try a little preplanning to save time—and gas money—before you hit the streets. See STEPS 1 and 2 in "How to Interview for a Job."

Dress to impress. When you are gathering job applications, be sure to dress well. You may actually find yourself speaking to the hiring manager or even asked to interview immediately. (See "How to Interview for a Job.")

Read all instructions. Be sure to carefully read all of the instructions before you begin filling anything out to ensure you understand the application questions.

Fill out the application. Use a ballpoint pen to neatly and honestly complete the application. Detail your prior work history in the specified location on the application. You will be asked to provide two or three references. (See "How to Ask for a Reference.") Describe your relationship and provide contact information for each reference.

Include supplementary documents. To verify your identity, the employer may ask to photocopy your driver's license or a state or federally issued ID.

Proofread. Make a good impression on the hiring manager by being sure your application is error free.

Turn in the application. Similar to when you picked up the application, dress appropriately in the event that you speak with the manager or are invited to interview for the position.

Fact or Fiction:

Spelling and grammar don't count on an application if the job involves physical labor.

Fiction. The fact is, a few spelling errors probably won't get your application tossed in the round file (trash can), but more than a few will. When in doubt, spell-check before filling in the blanks on an application.

Interview for a Job

YOU WILL NEED:

- Work résumé
- List of references
- Letters of recommendation
- Interview-appropriate clothing
- List of questions
- Thank-you note

TIME REQUIRED:

Varies, 10–30 minutes

*A*n interview is one step closer to the job you want! Nice work. Make sure you know what the company's dress code is or the general type or style of clothing worn at your potential workplace. It's usually better to be overdressed or more formal than too casual. If you get a chance to see how most employees in a company dress, it's good to follow suit . . .

and if it's suits, then literally wear a suit! Speak clearly and leave out any "ums," "yeahs," or "nahs" during the interview.

STEP **1**

Research the company. Gather information on the company's goals, work standards, and job qualifications to determine if you are a good fit for the work environment.

STEP **2**

Prepare yourself. Practice interviewing to ensure you are confident when it comes time to interview. Organize a professional portfolio that includes a copy of your résumé, list of references, and at least one letter of recommendation.

STEP **3**

Dress to impress. Choose interview-appropriate clothes. Dress to or slightly above the professional standards of the company.

STEP **4**

Stay focused. During your interview, listen carefully and answer clearly the interviewer's questions. Do not add unnecessary details to your answers.

STEP **5**

Ask good questions. Be prepared to ask your interviewer any professional question you need answered about the job, scheduled hours required to work, and performance expectations.

STEP **6**

Follow up. After your interview, send a thank-you note to the interviewer. This is your opportunity to remind them of your qualifications and what makes you a good fit for the job.

Wise Woman

"The best career advice to give to the young is, 'Find out what you like doing best and get someone to pay you for doing it.'"[4]

— Katharine Whitehorn, British journalist

Ask for a Raise

YOU WILL NEED:	TIME REQUIRED:
• Current pay research • List of your accomplishments that warrant a raise	30 minutes

So, you're thinking it's time you get a raise. Well, get in line—the long line. Nearly half of all workers believe they too are worth more, yet few do anything proactive to increase their pay. Most employees wait for the company to give out raises and feel undervalued when the boss doesn't. The best way to up your pay is to move from the long "waiting" line into the short "asking" line. If you are reasonably reliable, hardworking, and

have been on the job for more than a few months, it may be time to ask for a raise. Remember, those who don't ask, don't get.

STEP 1

Do your research. Determine how much others in your same position are earning.

STEP 2

Assess the workplace atmosphere. Do your best to determine if this is an appropriate time for the company to increase your pay.

STEP 3

Schedule a meeting. When asking your boss for a raise, you should ask in person. Never through a call, a text, or an email.

STEP 4

Prepare for your meeting. Outline your accomplishments and confidently list the reasons why the quality of your job performance is worth more than you are currently making.

STEP 5

Meet with your boss. In person, clearly present your request to your boss. Be prepared for whatever decision they make.

Did You Know?

Employers are required to pay their employees a minimum wage that meets or exceeds federal laws. Yet some states allow employers to include money received from service tips in an employee's minimum-wage calculation. When asking for a raise in the service industry, be sure to clarify how a raise will impact your hourly wage and tip totals.

Ask for a Promotion

YOU WILL NEED:

- Proven record of success in your current position
- Open need for position in the company
- Clear understanding of your professional strengths

TIME REQUIRED:

15 minutes

Want to know the best way to get promoted? It's no big rocket-science secret (unless you work for NASA). By definition a promotion is an upgrade, an advancement, or an elevated position. So the best way to work your way up to a promotion is to raise the bar on yourself. This means committing to do your very best in the job you already have. Once you are doing your work to near-perfect performance, your boss may see that you are ready to step up to the next challenge.

Consider the atmosphere. If the company is going through a period of layoffs, this may not be an appropriate time to approach your boss for a promotion.

Determine the need. If there is a job opening, you can apply for the job. If there is not an open position, determine the need of the company and how you are able to meet the need.

Evaluate your strengths. Highlight your contributions to the company and be prepared to present them to your boss.

Approach your boss. Schedule a face-to-face meeting with your boss to discuss your potential for a promotion.

Be specific. Outline a need in the company and how you can best fill that need. Anticipate questions from your boss and be prepared to defend your request.

Wait for a decision. Do not pressure your boss, but allow him or her time to come to a decision. Maintain a good attitude and work ethic regardless of the decision.

Wise Woman

"The joy is in the getting there. The beginning years of starting your business, the camaraderie when you're in the pit together, are the best years of your life."[5]

—Barbara Corcoran

Barbara Ann Corcoran is an American businesswoman, investor, speaker, business consultant, syndicated columnist, author, and television personality.

How to

Resign

YOU WILL NEED:
· Letter of resignation

TIME REQUIRED:
Minimum 2 weeks

*I*f the job is no longer working and you must move on, it's time to resign. Staying in a job too long when you know you are done with the position or company can cause problems. Try leaving on good terms and in good relationship with your co-workers and boss. Always remember that it's better to have a good connection than to burn a bridge.

STEP **1**

Put it in writing. Create a short professional letter of resignation. This letter should be clear, free from personal emotions, indicate a specific departure date, outline your achievements, and express gratitude to your boss and the company.

STEP **2**

Proofread your letter. Be sure your letter is free from all spelling and grammar errors.

STEP **3**

Turn in your letter. At least two weeks prior to your resignation date, personally present your letter of resignation to your boss and the human resources department. Keep a copy of the letter for your personal records.

STEP **4**

Ask for a recommendation. If appropriate, ask your boss for a personal recommendation that you can use in the future.

STEP **5**

Work to replace yourself. Aid in the process of finding your replacement and training them before you leave.

STEP **6**

Check into benefits. You may be entitled to benefits from the company upon your departure. Check with the human resources department to see if this is the case.

STEP **7**

Return company property. Prior to your departure, return all company-owned items to the appropriate departments. This will help to ensure that you leave on good terms.

Wise Woman

"There's a difference between giving up and knowing when you have had enough."

—Said by smart moms everywhere

Ask for a Reference

YOU WILL NEED:
- List of respectable people familiar with your performance
- Email addresses
- Phone numbers
- Computer with internet access

TIME REQUIRED:
30 minutes

It's a really bad idea to put someone down as a reference if you haven't asked them first. Putting someone on the spot like that could end up being a negative. Give your potential reference the chance to decide if they will give you a good reference and to be ready with something to say when their reference is called for. This will benefit you by keeping good relations with your reference and guarantee that your potential future employer will get a good reference for you.

Create a list. Write down a list of people who will give honest feedback about your past performance.

Consider email. Sending an email first can be the best way to request a reference because it doesn't put the receiver on the spot. If they agree to recommend you, good. If not, they can decline without the awkwardness of telling you no in person.

Draft an email. Write a simple straight-to-the-point message about the role you are seeking and your request for their recommendation. Do not ask, "Can you give me a reference?" Do ask something like, "Do you feel comfortable giving me a good reference?" Be sure to briefly answer these key questions: What is the role you are seeking? Why is this role important to you? When do you need to hear back with a yes or no about your reference request?

Proofread your request. Have somebody else proofread your reference request. Pick a proofreader who will tell you what you need to know about your writing skills and not simply what you want to hear.

Send the emails. Send each reference request individually. Do not send out a group email. Briefly personalize each request with something the reader will value about your relationship.

Follow up. When you hear back about your request, follow up with another email or, better yet, a phone call. Despite their answer of yes or no, thank the person for their thoughtful consideration.

Fact or Fiction:

People still send thank-you notes.

Fact. Americans spend between $7 billion and $8 billion on greeting cards each year. Second only to birthday cards, thank-you cards are given to millions of appreciated people each year.

4

Wealth & Money Management

Winning with money is simple—live on less than you make.

—RACHEL CRUZE, rachelcruze.com

*F*inancial phenom Rachel Cruze has been working to master money management since she was young. From age 15 she has stood on stage beside her cash-savvy dad, Dave Ramsey, teaching about the value of budgeting, saving, and spending wisely. If the family name Ramsey is new to you, they're the stay-out-of-debt, getting-out-of-debt, financial-stewardship gurus who actually practice what they teach.

Over the years Rachel has built a large following of money-wise women. Through bestselling books, blogs, vlogs, her website, and social media, she has coached millions of people to conquer their finances rather than be conquered by them. Since 2010 Rachel has been working with Ramsey Solutions, traveling the country, speaking to college students and young adults about money management. Her *Foundations in Personal Finance* is curriculum for high school and college-age students that is truly "on the money." The goal is for students to gain the knowledge about money that will help them practice good financial habits and earn a sound financial future. Rachel says that "the habits we form early in life will affect our future."[1]

Rachel's website is loaded with cash-managing information about budgeting, saving, and staying or getting out of debt. Her YouTube channel offers even more guidance for a positive-cash-flow kind of life. In her video "4 Common Sense Money Habits for Everyday Living," Rachel offers simple money principles that will help you get on track financially and stay out of debt. She sets viewers up for success by saying, "One of my favorite parts about personal finance is that it doesn't have to be complicated! You can win with money just by using common sense. So here are four commonsense money habits that you can start implementing today!"

1. Live on less than you make.
2. If you don't have the money, don't buy it.
3. Talk about money, even when it's hard.
4. Log into your bank account and know what's going on.[2]

Yet many young women will still argue that spending is so much more fun than saving. After all, most people get a kick out of buying something new. But who wants to be a slave to debt and live broke? Not the wise ones, that's for sure. Be a wise woman and take Rachel's wisdom to heart when she says, "Living with the idea that debt has to be a part of your life is going to keep you broke."[3] Also hear her well when she shares the guidance of her father's advice: "If you will live like no one else, later you can live and give like no one else."[4]

Recommended reading: *Love Your Life, Not Theirs* by Rachel Cruze

Create a Personal Budget

YOU WILL NEED:
· Lined paper
· Sharp pencil
· Calculator

TIME REQUIRED:
30 minutes

<u>STEP</u> **1**

Determine your income. List all the consistent ways you make money each month.

<u>STEP</u> **2**

Total your income. Add up the money earned and subtract any taxes you must pay. This is your total monthly income.

<u>STEP</u> **3**

List your expenses. Where do you spend your money each month? List everything. Yes, everything! Categorize if needed, but every penny spent must be accounted for!

Identify your fixed expenses. Review your list of expenses for things you can't live without. Fixed expenses are things you are committed to each month, month after month. Expenses like rent, utilities, insurance, and food should top this list.

Total your monthly fixed expenses. Add up your fixed expenses and this is your total monthly fixed expense budget.

Do the math. Subtract your fixed expenses from your income. If you have money left over, congratulations. Your budget is "in the black" because you are living "below your means." You can move to STEP 9. If you are out of cash, your budget is "in the red." You are living "above your means" and need to either increase your income or reduce your expenses.

> "Spend less than you make, and save more than you think you may need."
>
> —SHARON EMERSON,
> Senior Personal Finance
> Correspondent, CNBC

Identify your flexible expenses. Review your original expenses list for expenditures you can live without yet choose to buy.

Total your monthly flexible expenses. If you are spending "above your means," you'll need to reduce your flexible expenses (or increase your income) to get to your goal of being "in the black."

Watch your money. Keep an account of all your expenses. Cash, debit, and credit transactions need to be recorded and reviewed each month. This will help you stay accountable to where and why your money is being spent.

More Info

Have you included charitable giving in your monthly budget? Many financially savvy people give 10% or more of their income away each month. Start with what you know you can afford, and increase it as your budget and compassion allow.

Build a Savings Account

YOU WILL NEED:
- Income
- Savings account at a bank
- Personal budget
- Willpower

TIME REQUIRED:
1+ years

STEP 1

Create a personal budget. See "How to Create a Personal Budget."

STEP 2

Set a financial goal. Identify how much you want to save and by when you want it saved. This will require you to revisit your personal budget and make the changes needed to reprioritize some of your flexible spending as savings.

Pay off debt. If you owe others money, be sure to put first things first by paying off debt. Use the money you reprioritized in your budget for savings to pay back any debts. Not only will you be free from the burden of owing, but you will also be released from the additional expense of the debt's interest rate.

> "Money is only a tool. It will take you wherever you wish, but it will not replace you as the driver."
>
> —AYN RAND, Russian-American bestselling novelist

STEP **4**

Open a savings account. Take your first deposit to a reputable bank and open an interest-bearing savings account. *Interest-bearing* means the bank will pay you a set percentage of your account balance just for keeping your money in their bank. It's not much, but your money will grow over time.

STEP **5**

Keep to your budget. Now that you have included saving in your monthly budget, be sure to contribute to your savings account as planned before giving in to the temptation of an impulse purchase.

STEP **6**

Stay out of debt. Why buy when you can't afford it? If a purchase is not part of your budget, don't buy it. With the single swipe of a card, stroke of a pen, or click of a mouse, you can kill your savings.

STEP **7**

Repeat STEPS 5-6.

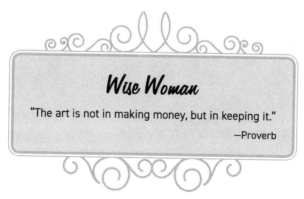

Wise Woman

"The art is not in making money, but in keeping it."

—Proverb

Manage a Credit Card Account

YOU WILL NEED:	TIME REQUIRED:
· Income	15 minutes per month
· Credit card	
· Personal budget	
· Willpower	

*A*merican consumers owe more than $905 billion in credit card debt. That's a lot of money owed and even more that will be paid once interest rates are calculated and collected. Properly managing a credit card keeps you from paying more than you owe. Owing money to a credit card company is like being enslaved to debt. The key to avoiding the bondage of debt is to not spend what you don't have. Despite how much you want to buy something, think of how much you don't want to be bound to debt. Think of it this way: The fun of building up debt is short lived, while the pain of tearing it back down again can last a lifetime.

STEP 1

Limit your choices. You do not need more than one credit card.

STEP 2

Know your credit card's terms and conditions. This includes your maximum credit line, interest rate, payment due date, and any transaction fees specific to your card.

STEP 3

Charge only if you must. Your credit card should be a last-resort payment option. Use it for emergencies when cash or debit payments are not an option. Daily budgeted expenses should not be paid with a credit card whenever possible. (See "How to Create a Personal Budget.")

STEP 4

Review your monthly statements. Always look over the statement of purchases. Compare the statement to the accounting of your monthly budget. Keep an eye open for any unauthorized charges or fees, as they may be a sign of credit card fraud. Credit card companies recommend cardholders check their account online a few times a month so that any unauthorized use of the card is caught ASAP.

STEP 5

Make your payments. Each month pay off your balance to avoid interest and service fees. Always pay before the due date to avoid late fees and any potential negative impact on your credit score.

Fact or Fiction:

The first credit card was made of leather.

Fiction. The fact is, the first credit card was most likely paper. Since then, credit cards or credit tokens have been made from metal coins, metal plates, fiber, paper, and plastic, but not leather.

Invest in the Future

YOU WILL NEED:
- Income
- Long-term investment account
- Patience

TIME REQUIRED:
30 minutes a month for the next 40+ years

Smart saving and investing: It's never too early to start, so the experts say. The younger you begin, the easier it is to make building your savings account a healthy habit. If you can save enough to not worry when your payday is, that's fantastic—it is a reward for your good work. Keep it up; it will serve you well in your future!

STEP 1

Begin with the end in mind. Think ahead to when you want to stop working. Most people set their sights on retiring around age 65 or older.

Earn an income. To invest money for tomorrow you need to earn money today. So get a job and set aside a percentage of your pay for investment.

STEP **3**

Pick an investment plan. Find a financial advisor who can guide you to a long-term investment plan that takes advantage of compound interest.

STEP **4**

Start early. The key to maximizing your money is to start investing as soon as possible. Here's what will happen to an investment earning 10% that is compounded yearly:

$10,000 invested at age 20 will be $728,905 by age 65
$10,000 invested at age 25 will be $452,593 by age 65
$10,000 invested at age 30 will be $281,024 by age 65
$10,000 invested at age 40 will be $108,347 by age 65

Wise Woman

"Let's say you bought a Starbucks coffee every day, from age 20 to age 60. Which sounds like a lot but some people do that, and you spend $5 every day. Instead of spending that $5 if you had invested it every day, or every month, the total will be $817,000! . . . It's crazy to think what happens when you invest instead of spend money."[5]

—Rachel Cruze

Live Debt-Free

YOU WILL NEED:	TIME REQUIRED:
• Income	From now on
• Self-control	
• Patience	

*W*ith banks and credit card companies offering a way to build credit, these roads often lead people down into a dark and bottomless pit of debt. Debt is a trap from which it can be extremely difficult to recover. Spending only the money you make is the best way to stay out of debt. Not so easy, you say? With a credit history needed to purchase things like a car or a house, it does seem impossible to live without a credit card. Staying out of debt doesn't mean you don't have a credit card; it means you know when and how to use one.

STEP 1

Earn an income. Financial independence begins when you earn your own income.

STEP 2

Value your money. Money is a tool, not a toy. You work hard to earn it, so look for ways to make your money work hard for you.

STEP 3

Know your needs. Know the difference between needs and wants. Don't spend money on something you want if it doesn't leave you with enough money to spend on what you need.

STEP 4

Create a personal budget. Telling your money where to go beats wondering where it went. (See "How to Create a Personal Budget.")

STEP **5**

Pay cash. Cash is a very visible way to keep track of your money. Spending $60 out of the $100 you have leaves you with exactly what you have. No guessing or pretending, there's only $40 remaining.

STEP **6**

Save. Work your budget with the goal of your income being greater than your expenses. Deposit the remaining money into your savings and long-term investment account.

STEP **7**

Don't spend what you don't have. Stay away from buying and carrying a balance on a credit card. (See "How to Manage a Credit Card Account.")

Wise Woman

"You're never powerful in life until you're powerful over your money."[6]

—Suze Orman, author, financial advisor, and TV host

5

Health & Beauty

*A little makeup
and styled hair
should never be used
to outshine the beauty
from within.*
—ERICA CATHERMAN

*T*aking good care of yourself doesn't mean you need to spend hours in the bathroom and hundreds of dollars on beauty products. Finding a health and beauty system that you can maintain consistently will help keep your hair, skin, teeth, and body looking and feeling healthy.

My friend and personal stylist Kelly Grathwohl has been a consultant since 2000. Surrounded by women at work, having two sisters, and raising a daughter of her own, Kelly knows the struggles girls and women go through daily. When it comes to her clients' needs for hair and makeup, Kelly says choosing healthy and natural is best! "With makeup, less is more. Sometimes I see young girls coming in with a thick layer of makeup on their face and it just looks so unnatural. Keep it clean. When just starting out with makeup products try clear mascara, lip gloss rather than lipstick, maybe a blemish stick for outbreaks or tinted moisturizer. Really, no foundation should be necessary . . . maybe powder."[1]

Kelly goes on to emphasize, "Take care of your hair, nails, and skin with good, natural products. Acrylic nails are expensive and damaging to your natural nails. Drink lots of water or fruit-infused water, stay away from sugar. This will especially help your skin but will also benefit your hair and nails."

It takes years to become a well-respected professional stylist like Kelly. Thus she knows her wise advice of keeping your look simple and healthy is more than a passing fad. The most beautiful look a woman can wear is confidence in herself.

Properly Wash Your Hair

YOU WILL NEED:
· Water
· Shampoo
· Conditioner
· Absorbent cotton towel

TIME REQUIRED:
5–10 minutes depending on length, thickness, and texture of hair

As every girl knows, her hair needs to be washed. And you've been washing your hair your entire life—so what more is there to learn? Well, sometimes the *way* a girl washes her hair can cause problems. Girls going through puberty should be aware that their hair may become oilier during this awkward stage of life. Proper washing, not necessarily more washing, is one important way to keep your hair feeling silky and not slippery. Root to tip, your hair needs regular cleansing and thorough rinsing. Ask the person you trust to cut and care for your hair which products will work best for your hair type, the best washing methods, and how often you should wash your locks. Don't be afraid to let them know your budget, as it can be easy to overspend on expensive hair products.

STEP 1

Wet hair. Completely wet your hair from root to tip.

STEP 2

Shampoo. Use the directed amount of shampoo (either on the shampoo bottle or recommended by your stylist), first putting it in the palm of your hand. Create a lather in your hands with the shampoo and apply to your hair starting at the roots. Make sure to get all the way to your scalp through your entire head of hair and use your fingertips to massage the shampoo onto your scalp.

STEP 3

Rinse. Completely rinse the shampoo from your scalp and hair. This may take longer than you think, but leaving shampoo residue on your scalp or in your hair can cause irritation, an oily look, or flat-looking hair.

Condition. Add a small amount of conditioner to your palm. Spread the conditioner on both hands and apply to your hair starting at the tips. Don't apply to the scalp unless your stylist thinks your hair needs it. This can be a good time to comb out your hair, if needed.

Rinse. Completely rinse the conditioner from your hair. Squeeze excess water out of your hair.

Towel dry. Use an absorbent cotton towel to dry your hair as much as possible. Gently squeeze your hair in the towel to reduce friction and possible hair breakage. This will reduce the time you spend with a hairdryer (if you use one), potentially reducing heat damage to your hair! Do not twist wet hair up into a towel for a prolonged time, as the weight of the towel pulls at your roots when your hair is most vulnerable to breakage.

Fact or Fiction:

Coloring your hair with Kool-Aid is cool.

Fiction. Color not intended for use on hair can do serious damage to the hair follicle. Yes, it all grows out, but your hair can end up looking super shabby, not chic, when not using a pro to help with hair color.

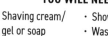
Shave Your Legs

YOU WILL NEED:

- Shaving cream/ gel or soap
- Body lotion
- New razor
- Shower or bathtub
- Washcloth
- Tissue for bleeding

TIME REQUIRED:

5 minutes

*H*airy legs. Some people don't have a problem with them. It would be nice to not have to take the time to rid legs of hair, but most women prefer to lose the leg locks. If you're going to shave, take care to avoid nicks and cuts, as these can be painful and tend to bleed a lot (especially around the ankles). A good razor is helpful in not accidentally shearing off long strips of skin. Shaving cream or gel can also help that razor glide smoothly over your legs with less chance of blood.

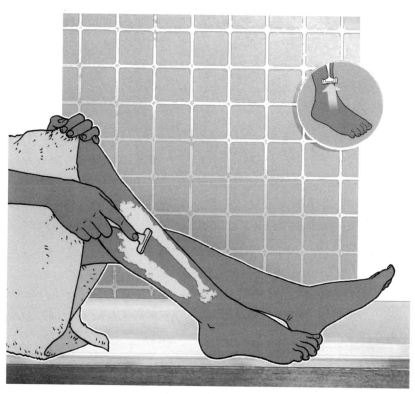

Step into a bathtub or shower—either will do. Run warm water in the shower or to fill the bath.

Wet your legs. Wet your legs for several minutes to soften your leg hair.

Apply shaving cream or soap. Squirt a golf-ball-sized amount of shaving cream or soap into the palm of your hand. Apply a thin, even layer over the area you will shave.

Shave. Applying light but firm pressure with the razor, first shave in the same direction as the hair grows, especially if the hair is long or thick. Then start just above the ankle and shave up toward the knee. Be careful around the ankle and knee to avoid nicking yourself.

Rinse your razor. Use the warm water from the bath or shower to rinse your razor after a few strokes. This keeps the space between the blades from getting clogged.

Shave the area around your knee. Glide your razor over your unflexed knee and then give your knee a little flex. Be careful to take shorter strokes with the razor, and don't hesitate to go over an area from a couple different directions.

Check your work. Wash away any excess shaving cream and examine your leg for hairs that remain unshaved. Check the knee and ankle line. If needed, you can reapply shaving cream and re-shave any missed hairs.

Rinse. With a wet washcloth or running water, wipe or rinse your leg clean. Reexamine your leg for nicks that may bleed slightly. Simply apply a small piece of tissue to the nick. This will help stop the bleeding. Just remember to remove the tissue before leaving the house.

STEP **9**

Repeat STEPS 3-8 on the other leg.

Bonus STEP

Moisturize. Once done and dried off, apply your favorite body lotion for smooth skin!

Fact or Fiction:

Shaving makes hair grow back thicker and faster.

Fiction. The fact is, shaving doesn't affect hair growth or thickness. Hair may appear to be thicker simply because cut ends are blunt and more obvious.

Shave under Your Arms

YOU WILL NEED:

- Shaving cream/ gel or soap
- New razor
- Shower or bathtub
- Hairy armpits
- Deodorant or antiperspirant

TIME REQUIRED:

3 minutes

Some people don't mind hairy pits, while others would rather go hairless under the arms. If you choose to lose the pit hair, it's fairly quick and easy compared to shaving legs. Still, pay close attention to get all the hairs, and remember to always use quality soap, cream, or gel and a good razor.

STEP 1

Step into a bathtub or shower—either will do. Run warm water in the shower or to fill the bath.

STEP 2

Wet your armpits for a minute or so. This helps soften the hairs in preparation for shaving.

STEP 3

Apply soap, shaving cream, or gel. Apply a thin, even layer of shaving cream, soap, or gel to an armpit. Cover the entire armpit area.

STEP 4

Shave. First shave in the same direction your armpit hair grows. Then after a few swipes, go against the direction the hair grows to get a close, smooth shave.

STEP 5

Rinse the razor. After a few swipes with the razor you will need to rinse the razor. A clogged razor makes it difficult to get a close shave.

STEP 6

Rinse your armpit. Clean off any remaining soap, shaving cream, or gel along with the shaved hair.

STEP 7

Repeat STEPS 3-6 on the other armpit.

STEP 8

Apply deodorant or antiperspirant. It's good to apply a daily dose of deodorant/antiperspirant to clean armpits. To avoid irritating your freshly shaved skin, try waiting 10 minutes after shaving before applying.

Antiperspirants vs. Deodorants

Antiperspirants—According to the "sweatperts" at the University of North Carolina's Department of Dermatology, the key weapon used to combat underarm wetness is aluminum. Antiperspirants help block sweat by introducing aluminum ions into the skin-level cells of the sweat glands in your armpit. When your glands begin to push water out, aluminum ions react with your perspiration, causing the cells to swell and squeezing the sweat ducts closed.

Deodorants—Classified as a cosmetic by the US Food and Drug Administration (FDA), deodorant is little more than an armpit air freshener formulated to mask the foul-smelling body odor all humans emit. Yep, everybody has a unique "odortype." Your odortype is a mix of environmental factors, including when you showered last, if you used soap in that shower, what you eat, how much water you drink, and the DNA you inherited from your parents. There is no escaping the smell of your genetics, but you do control how often you shower and what you choose to eat. So keep both your body and food fresh for a better-smelling tomorrow.

Apply Hair-Styling Product

YOU WILL NEED:
- Clean hair
- Hair product (mousse, gel, and/or sprays)

TIME REQUIRED:
1–5 minutes

*I*t's been said that a woman's hair is her crown. Some girls do theirs up daily like a jeweled tiara. Others like their locks to fall in a more natural way. Although hair product is not always needed to achieve your perfect look, sometimes a little gel or mousse will hold your style strong, straight, curly, or spiked a little longer. But with so many hair product options available, how does a girl choose? Start by knowing the look you like, find a product made for that style, and give it a go.

STEP 1

Select your product. Choose a mousse, gel, or spray depending on what you want your hair to feel like when done. Mousse or mousse

sprays often give volume and some hold. Gel will give you hold but can look wet or greasy if not dried properly. Sprays are a mix, and the description on the bottle will let you know if it's for volume, shine, or hold. Pick the one with your desired outcome, or just as with products for washing your hair, the person you trust to cut and care for your hair can be a good source of information for appropriate styling products.

STEP **2**

Read the directions carefully. Yep, take a minute to read the directions—like applying to dry hair, damp hair, or fully wet hair, applying at the roots or the tips, or using in conjunction with another product.

STEP **3**

Apply product. Follow the directions on the bottle.

STEP **4**

Style your hair. Have fun! You can look into types of hair dryers, curling irons, flat irons, different types of brushes, rollers, and on and on. Or just brush and go!

CAUTION

Flat irons and curling irons can damage your hair, leading to breakage and split ends.

Dry ironing: Ironing dry hair causes cracking along the edges of the hair follicle, which can lead to chipping.

Wet ironing: Ironing wet hair causes the moisture to burst out in little steam explosions. This causes a bubbling and buckling of the hair follicle that appears as tiny hair blisters under magnification.

SOLUTION

Reduce iron damage by using conditioners formulated specifically to protect against heat. Of course, not using an iron is the best solution.

Wash Your Hands Properly

YOU WILL NEED:
- Running water (warm or cold)
- Soap
- Clean towel

TIME REQUIRED:
1 minute

Curious minds at the Wright Patterson Medical Center in Dayton, Ohio, did the research and discovered these filthy facts. The #1 germ-ridden thing we handle is an average $1 bill. Additional top touches on the disgusting list include light switches, keyboards, cell phones, and toilet seats. Sound familiar? Avoiding these contaminated conveniences is next to impossible, yet there is one highly effective way to keep clean. Wash your hands. Regularly.

STEP **1**

Wet hands. Under clean running water, wet your hands up to your wrists.

STEP 2

Apply soap. Bar or liquid soap will do.

STEP 3

Lather hands. Vigorously rub your hands together to create soap lather from your fingertips to wrists.

STEP 4

Scrub hands. For at least 20 seconds, scrub the back of your hands, between your fingers, and under your nails.

STEP 5

Rinse hands. Under running water, rinse the soap lather from your hands.

STEP 6

Dry hands. Use a clean towel or air to dry your hands.

STEP 7

Turn off water. If possible, use your drying towel to turn water off.

More Info

Knowing when to wash is key to maintaining good health. Here are some of the top times you want to be sure to have clean hands.

Before—food preparation, eating, brushing your teeth, caring for a sick friend, treating a wound, washing your face, unloading the dishwasher, holding a baby

After—food preparation, caring for a sick friend, treating a wound, using the bathroom, changing a diaper, blowing your nose, coughing, sneezing, feeding your pet, petting your pet, scooping your pet's mess, taking out the trash

Freshen Bad Breath

YOU WILL NEED:

- Toothbrush and toothpaste
- Floss
- Drinking water
- Sugar-free cinnamon gum (or your favorite sugar-free flavor)

TIME REQUIRED:

2 minutes

*B*ad breath stinks—literally! Proper dental hygiene, including flossing (because there's nothing like leaving rotting food between your bicuspids), a healthy diet, hydration, and regular dental visits are all helpful to keeping your mouth smelling good. Having a clean mouth prepares you to talk to anyone at any time with no concern of a stench floating from your mouth to their nose. If you're still concerned about your mouth, keep some mints or gum on hand to temporarily freshen your breath.

121

Brush your teeth. Get in the habit of brushing your pearly whites at least twice a day. Give them a cleaning for two minutes. One minute on your uppers and one minute on your lowers.

Clean your tongue. Stick out your tongue and look in the mirror. What color is it? If it isn't a clean, fleshy pink color, use your toothbrush to scrape the surface clean. Dentists recommend brushing your tongue every time you brush your teeth to help prevent bacteria from building up in your mouth.

Floss. You will be surprised how much food jams down between your pearly whites. Lack of flossing can be a leading cause of bad breath due to decaying food particles.

Drink more water. Water keeps your mouth hydrated and helps produce saliva. Saliva is bacteria's worst enemy because it contains germ-slaying antiseptic and enzymes. Less bacteria in your mouth means less of their "waste" is deposited between your teeth. Their digested waste is just like your digested waste. It stinks. So help flush it away by drinking water.

Chew sugar-free gum. Chewing gum encourages the production of saliva. But stay away from the super-sugary gums. Bacteria thrive on sugar.

Eat healthy. Two types of food can really make your breath reek. Smelly food like garlic, onions, cheese, and coffee pack a pungent punch. You will also want to cut out junk foods high in sugar and fat. Bacteria thrive on sugar and fat.

Did You Know?

Smell your floss after flossing. Seriously. If your floss stinks it's because bacteria are depositing their "deposits" along your gum line. These microscopic-sized "number twos" cause gum disease, and that gum disease stinks. No brand of trendy gum can fix that kind of dirty mouth. So what's the solution? Floss. Every day. Your mouth and your floss should smell better in about a week. If they don't, talk with your dentist—from a safe distance, please.

Wear Perfume

*A*pply too much perfume and people will smell you before they see you. This is not good. You want those who get close enough to notice your perfume to think, "She smells nice." Which is much better than, "Yuck! Did she take a bath in that stuff?" When it comes to wearing perfume, less is more. In fact, it's best to not wear perfume every day. That and maybe try a new scent every few months, unless you want to be remembered as the one-scent wonder—then make sure it's a good one!

Wear one scent. Make sure you are not wearing any other scented products. Lotions, body wash, or deodorant with their own distinctive scents will likely clash with the smell of your perfume. Just because they are the same brand doesn't mean they are supposed to be worn together. It's best to pick one.

Remove cap. Carefully open perfume bottle.

Apply perfume. Pick a place to apply a light amount of perfume to your skin. The temperature of your skin interacts with the release of the scent in your perfume. Some women prefer the pulse points, like behind the ears, on the wrists, the crook of the elbow, even behind the knees. One or two drops or sprays is all you need. Three can be potent and should be your absolute maximum.

IMPORTANT

Don't apply directly to your clothes. Perfume can stain fabric and the smell can change depending on the laundry products used to clean your clothes.

Recap perfume. You don't want to spill this stuff.

Did You Know?

Counterfeiting perfume is big business. It can be difficult to sniff out the fake, as imitators are really good at making the packaging, bottle, and scents very close to the real thing. But counterfeit perfumes use ingredients not certified by the FDA. The imposter product can produce an unattractive rash on your skin or even a health-threatening allergic reaction. Other noses might not know you're wearing a knockoff perfume, but your skin may not be able to hide the truth. So keep it real by buying from reputable stores and never trust a deal that smells too good to be true.

Wash Your Face

YOU WILL NEED:
- Warm water
- Clean washcloth and towel
- Face soap or cleanser

TIME REQUIRED:
5 minutes

*A*cne. It's a dirty word, especially for teenagers. As people go through puberty, they are often hit with increased levels of oil on the skin, more sweat, and hormones in general. The combination can lead to more ZITS! Avoid them by keeping your skin clean and eating foods that won't increase oil levels on your face. When you make washing your face and neck a part of your routine every morning, evening, and after any physical activity that causes you to sweat, you'll be doing yourself a real acne-fighting favor.

STEP 1

Use a clean washcloth. Wet it with warm water.

STEP 2

Hold the warm washcloth to your face and neck. Continue this application for about one minute. This will loosen surface dirt and open your skin pores.

STEP 3

Apply the mild soap or cleanser to your face and neck. Use a mild, non-irritating, alcohol-free skin product. Apply on a soft washcloth and gently scrub your face, using a circular motion. Do not press too hard, as this could scuff the surface of your face, and do not scrub too vigorously, as this can irritate and dry out your skin. Dry skin is more likely to trigger a rash and increase oil production.

STEP 4

Rinse your face. Use warm water to rinse all soap from your face and neck.

STEP 5

Don't touch! Seriously. Your hands are covered with bacteria, and bacteria love to infest your face. "I don't touch my face!" you say. Really? Do you rest your elbow on your desk and your chin on your hand? Do you scratch, push, pick, or pinch at your pimples? Do you wash your hands often . . . like every hour? Yeah, that's what I thought. Now stop touching your face.

STEP 6

Eat and drink better. What goes in must come out, and that includes through your skin. Your hormone balances react to your diet; since acne is also linked to hormone imbalances, it's a good idea to watch what you eat. If you devour greasy foods high in saturated fats, salt, and sugar, your body reacts by jacking up or turning down hormone balances. Skin is the body's largest organ, and it is supersensitive to your hormones. When you eat junk food, you can get junk skin. It's best to avoid deep-fried food, processed food, fast food, and energy drinks packed with ingredients difficult to pronounce. Your best practice is to drink fewer manufactured beverages and more of the natural stuff, aka water.

Fact or Fiction:

Tanning zaps zits.

Fiction. The fact is, UV rays from the sun or tanning beds damage your skin and can actually make acne blemishes worse.

Trim Your Fingernails

YOU WILL NEED:
- Sharp, clean nail cutter
- Nail file
- Wastebasket

TIME REQUIRED:
5 minutes

*N*o biting! Did you know that the space under your fingernails harbors double the count of germs and bacteria that is found on any other exposed place on your body? Keep your mouth clean and your nails properly trimmed with these easy steps.

STEP **1**

Soak your fingernails. In warm water, soak your fingernails before cutting. This finger bath softens the nails, making them easier to trim.

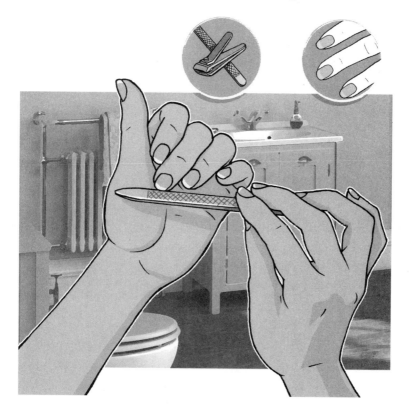

Examine your nails. Keep an eye out for hangnails and any cuticle damage that may lead to an infection or nail damage.

Cut your nails. Over a wastebasket, use a sharp, clean nail cutter to snip your nails straight across until they show a nice thin, even line of white at the end of the nail.

File your nails. Once your nails have dried, use a nail file to smooth the edges. Uneven or jagged nails look sloppy and can catch on clothes, causing nails to tear or break.

Do a final inspection. Give your nails a final inspection to ensure each is the same length and shape and nice-n-smooth. Clip and file each until all of your fingernails look the same. When they do, you're done. Now repeat the same process on your toenails.

Did You Know?

Fingernails grow faster than toenails, and the nail of a woman's index finger grows faster than her pinky fingernail.

Care for Your Feet

YOU WILL NEED:

- Soap, washcloth, towel
- Sharp, clean nail cutter
- Nail file
- Skin moisturizer
- Wastebasket

TIME REQUIRED:

5 minutes

*P*edicures at a nail salon are awesome but cost cash that may not be in the budget. A home pedicure can be just as good and as elaborate as you want. Here is a simple way to have summertime, flip-flop ready, good-looking feet!

STEP 1

Soak your feet. Fill a tub with enough warm water to soak your feet.

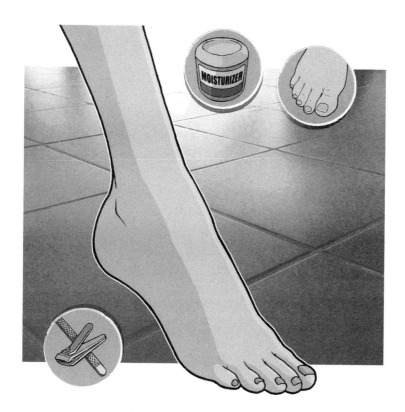

Wash your feet. Using soap and a washcloth, scrub your feet. Get down between each toe and under the nails. Dry each foot with a towel.

Examine your nails. Look at each toe's nail, keeping an eye out for hangnails and any cuticle damage that could lead to an infection.

Cut your toenails. Over a wastebasket, use a sharp, clean nail cutter to snip your nails so they show a nice thin, even line of white at the end of the nail. Cut them nearly straight across instead of curved to avoid ingrown toenails.

File your nails. Once your nails are dry, use a nail file to smooth the edges. Uneven or jagged toenails look sloppy and can tear or break easily.

Moisturize. Work the skin moisturizer into your skin from the ankle down to your toes. Let the moisturizer absorb before putting on your socks.

Did You Know?

We were made to move. According to scientists, our bodies are good to go for about 12 miles a day. Not only can our feet handle the distance, our brains crave the oxygen exercise provides. So, get up and get a-moving, you smart girl.[2]

Apply Nail Polish

YOU WILL NEED:

- Clean & trimmed nails
- Old hand towel or paper towel
- Nail polish
- Nail polish remover
- Cotton swabs
- Hair dryer or fan (optional)

TIME REQUIRED:
15–20 minutes

It's always nice to treat yourself to a mani-pedi at your favorite salon. But between those special occasions, the cost of touch-ups or full color change can quickly add up. Applying your own polish at home can be a bit challenging at first, but with a little practice you'll learn the tricks to a beautifully and personally applied shine. Soon you won't need a trip to the salon to show off those gorgeous fingers and toes.

STEP **1**

Clean and trim your nails. (See "How to Trim Your Fingernails" or "How to Care for Your Feet.")

Lay out the old hand towel or paper towel. This helps protect the surface you are working on and prevent messes.

Apply polish. When painting your nails, it's best to start on the pinky finger/toe and work your way to your thumb/big toe (less chance of hitting a nail and messing up the polish). Be careful not to overload the brush with paint and smoothly draw the brush from the cuticle to the tip of the nail. Let the brush fan a little to cover more nail. Make slow and careful brush strokes near the sides of the nail bed so you don't get polish on your skin. Work on keeping the brush on the nail so you'll have less to touch up.

Apply a second coat. After waiting a minimum of two minutes, repeat STEP 3.

Let nails dry completely. This can take a while, so practice your patience and don't smudge the work you just did on your nails. Maybe try a cool hair dryer or sit in front of a fan to let the polish set.

Clean up the skin and cuticles around your nails. Using a cotton swab dipped in nail polish remover, carefully "erase" the polish that may have made its way onto your skin.

Did You Know?

Nail polish originated in China around 3000 BC, but it wasn't until the 1930s that the polish we use today was developed with chemistry!

6

Clothes & Fashion

My mission in life is not merely to survive, but to thrive; and to do so with some passion, some compassion, some humor, and some style.[1]

—MAYA ANGELOU, American poet, memoirist, and civil rights activist

What is your mission in life? To look good, be good, or both? From the inspiration of Maya Angelou's mission statement, we learn life is to be lived in "thrive" mode. This is true when the good in you is worn from the inside out. Your passion, compassion, and personal style is the finest wardrobe you wear! And think about how diverse styles can be. It's a good thing not everyone needs to dress and look alike. That would be boring, and you're not a boring girl. Instead, focus on developing your own personal look and style. In turn, what you wear, how you wear it, and when you choose to wear it are all outward expressions of your inward confidence and consideration of others.

Let's start with your style confidence. Remember back when you used to play dress-up? How did that make you feel? Good chance you felt confident in the character your outfit represented. American fashion designer and businesswoman Kate Spade said, "Playing dress-up begins at age five and never truly ends."[2] No longer a little girl, you are a woman in the making, and the outfits you dress up in now should reflect the confidence within, rather than give you the confidence you require. As Anne Klein stated, "Clothes aren't going to change the world, the women who wear them will."[3]

Choosing what to wear and where you wear it is a measure of your style consideration. This can get tricky when the outfit you want to wear could clash with where you need to be today. If you are going to a wedding, are you dressed for a wedding? If you're headed to the beach, then wear beach clothes. Going out with friends, great . . . Have fun and dress appropriately. Just remember: Wearing designer clothes doesn't necessarily mean you have style. Whereas a woman who dresses with confidence and consideration will always be in style.

Wash Laundry

YOU WILL NEED:
- Dirty clothes
- Washing machine
- Laundry detergent
- Fabric softener (optional)

TIME REQUIRED:
Up to 2 hours

*J*ust because it looks clean doesn't mean it *is* clean. Clothes get "dirty" when they trap dust, spills, dirt, and sweat in their fibers. One reason your favorite outfit turns from looking good to smelling foul is because your body naturally excretes two types of perspiration. *Eccrine* is "normal" sweat and is mostly water. *Apocrine* is stress sweat, a gummy mix of ammonia, carbohydrates, proteins, and fatty acids. The bacteria that live on your skin and in your clothing enjoy feasting on both sweat types but really prefer apocrine. In thanks for their free meal, bacteria emit a sour

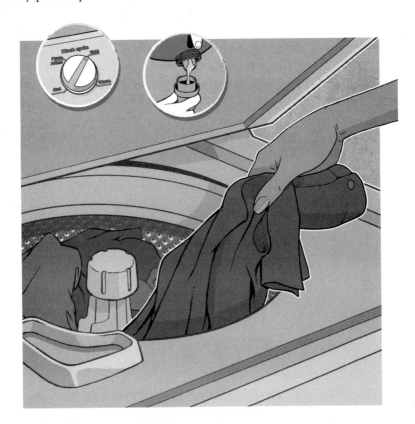

odor. That's what you smell wafting into the air from the dirty laundry pile. So follow this simple three-step rule to keep your clothes looking and smelling clean: (1) wear it, (2) wash it, and (3) put it away.

STEP 1

Separate clothes. Always read the label on your clothes to see if they are dry-clean only, hand-wash, or require being washed on a gently cycle. If not otherwise indicated, sort your clothes of like colors (darks vs. lights) to be washed in separate loads.

STEP 2

Load the washing machine. Place one load into the washing machine—darks only, lights only, or a hot wash only.

STEP 3

Select wash options. Set the wash options to match the type of material you are washing. Whites/sanitary, normal, heavy, and easy care are common settings.

IMPORTANT

The wash option for WHITES usually uses HOT water. Clothes can shrink in hot water, so reset the wash temperature to WARM or COLD if this is a concern.

STEP 4

Add laundry detergent. Read the label on the detergent package. Add the proper measurement to the washing machine. Liquid and powder detergents may need to be added differently, so read packaging instructions carefully.

IMPORTANT

Do NOT use regular detergent in a High Efficiency (HE) washer as it can damage the machine. HE detergent is clearly labeled on the product's packaging.

STEP 5

Start washer. Once clothes, detergent, and any fabric softener have been added, close the washer's door and start the machine.

IMPORTANT

Once the wash cycle is complete, remove clothes promptly to avoid mildew.

Types of Laundry Detergents

Powder—Dissolves in wash water. Less expensive
than liquid detergents.

Liquid—Pre-dissolved. Can be used to pre-treat stains
on clothes.

HE liquid—No/low suds required in high-efficiency
and front-load washers.

Fabric Check

Some fabrics shrink in hot water. When exposed to heat,
wool and cotton fibers can change shape. This results
in shorter sleeves, high-water pants, and that overall
one-size-too-small look you'll want to avoid.

Dry Laundry

YOU WILL NEED:
· Clothes from washer
· Dryer
· Dryer sheets (optional)

TIME REQUIRED:
30 minutes to 1.5 hours

When in doubt, hang it out . . . out to dry, that is. That sweater you love fits just right! Now that you have run it through the delicate cycle in the wash, what's the best way to dry it? There are so many settings on laundry machines today, and not all of them match what the fabric care tags on your clothes recommend. If you want a near-guarantee that a piece of clothing won't shrink, hang it up or smooth it out over a drying rack and keep it looking good and fitting great! All other laundry can be put in the dryer.

Clear the lint trap. Pull out and clean the dryer's lint trap to assure proper airflow and dryer efficiency. Lint traps are located close to the cycle option controls or just inside the dryer's door.

STEP **2**

Load the dryer. Move just-washed clothes from the washing machine into the dryer. Don't let wet clothes sit in the washer, as the scent of mildew will set in and no "Summer Breeze" dryer sheet will fix that.

STEP **3**

Add a dryer sheet (optional). A dryer sheet softens fabrics and prevents clothes from clinging together from the static electricity produced during tumble-drying.

STEP **4**

Select dry options. Set the dryer's options to match the type of fabrics you are drying.

IMPORTANT

The dryer's cycle options include a temperature setting. Clothes can shrink during a hot drying cycle. Adjust the temperature control to a cooler setting if this is a concern.

STEP **5**

Start the dryer. Once clothes and dryer sheet have been added, close the dryer's door and start the machine. Heavier weight fabrics and fuller loads take longer to dry.

STEP **6**

Once dry, remove clothes. Most dryers give you a few minutes of "fluff dry" before they stop tumbling. If you have clothing that you don't want to wrinkle, pull the clothes out of the dryer before the cycle stops and hang or fold them.

Did You Know?

According to FEMA's US Fire Administration National Fire Data Center, there are an estimated 2,900 dryer-related fires in residential buildings each year. Dust, fiber, and lint-clogged dryer vents are the leading cause of ignition. These dryer fires result in an estimated 5 deaths, 100 injuries, and $35 million in property losses annually.

Iron a Button-Down Shirt

YOU WILL NEED:
- Clean clothes
- Iron
- Ironing board
- Water
- Hangers

TIME REQUIRED:
8 minutes

*W*rinkles are a reality of any wardrobe, no matter what you do to prevent them. Even a fresh-out-of-the-dryer button-down shirt may require an ironing to achieve the crisp look you want. Take the time to iron out those wrinkles and people will notice.

STEP 1

Open the ironing board. In a space close to an electrical outlet, open and stand the ironing board.

Prep the iron. Add water to the steam reservoir, plug the iron in, and select the proper fabric temperature setting. (DO NOT overheat the iron, as this can burn and ruin your shirt.) Set iron upright until it is warmed up.

Iron the collar. Smooth the collar top side down on the ironing board. Iron the collar from the edge to the neck seam before flipping to check for smoothness.

Press the shoulders and yoke of shirt. Open the shirt and lay it inside down, flat on the ironing board. Position the shoulders over the narrow side of the ironing board. Iron the fabric from the lower edge of the collar down and across to the top of each sleeve. Move the shirt as needed to reach the full span of the shoulders.

Press the cuffs. With the same approach as taken to iron the collar, press each cuff.

Smooth the sleeves. Lay one sleeve flat on the ironing board with the bottom seam toward you. Press the sleeve with the iron from the top of the sleeve to the cuff. If desired, iron in a crease along the top edge of the sleeve. Turn the shirt and repeat on the other sleeve.

Flatten the body panels. Reposition the shirt so the collar is toward the narrow end of the board. Starting at the top of the shirt, iron down the buttonhole side to the shirttail. Turn the shirt and press the back panel. Turn again to press the button side of the shirt.

Button and hang. Place the shirt on a hanger and button the top button. Hang the shirt.

Clean up. Unplug the iron, wait for it to cool, and empty any remaining water from the reservoir. Put the iron and ironing board away.

More Info

If using an unfamiliar or old iron, test it first on an old towel or at least on the ironing board cover. Mineral deposits will sometimes come out with the steam and ruin your clothing. To minimize mineral deposits from building up in your iron, try using *distilled* water in the steam reservoir.

Iron Slacks/Pants

*W*alking with pride includes knowing you have the confidence needed to iron yourself a crisp pair of slacks/pants. The look will serve you well when wearing something other than your favorite pair of jeans and will be the skill you need when you want to dress to impress.

STEP **1**

Read the tag. Stitched into the waist seam of your slacks is a tag with cleaning instructions. Check these instructions for a proper iron temperature and steam setting. If steam is required, add water to the iron's reservoir prior to turning it on, and heat it up.

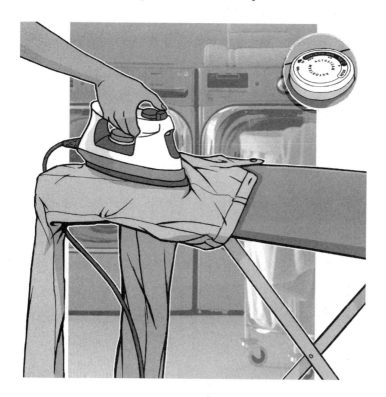

Lay them down. Holding your slacks by the waistband, shake them out a few times to remove any major creases. Make sure the pockets are tucked in properly. Holding the waistband, fold your slacks so one leg is on top of the other. The seams and creases of your slacks should line up.

Iron the legs. Lay the legs on the ironing board. After the iron is hot, start at the top of your slacks and slowly run the iron over the top leg to eliminate any wrinkles. When the top leg is smooth, carefully flip it up and repeat with the bottom leg. Now fold the top leg back down and make sure the creases are in the same place on each leg.

Flip and repeat. Turn your slacks over so the recently ironed side is facing down. Repeat STEPS 2 and 3 with the other side of your slacks.

Iron the waist. Now slide the waist over the narrow end of the board and iron. Rotate the slacks, ironing the upper legs too, until everything is all nicely pressed.

Turn your iron off and take care of the clothing. Unplug the iron, wait for it to cool, and empty any remaining water from the reservoir. Put the iron and ironing board away. If you are not going to wear your slacks immediately, hang or fold them neatly.

Did You Know?

Ironing your slacks is real science at work. The act of pressing the cloth with a hot iron loosens the molecular chains that hold polymer fibers together, stretches them slightly, and causes them to retain their flattened shape as the fabric cools.

Care for Leather Shoes or Boots

YOU WILL NEED:		TIME REQUIRED:
• Towel or newspaper to ensure easy cleanup • Shoe polish: comes in liquid or wax form	• Horsehair shine brush • Soft cloth • Pair of leather shoes or boots	30–45 minutes

So you saved up and got your favorite pair of shoes or boots. If they are leather and you have them for a season, you may want to think about giving them a polish. This will protect the leather and keep them looking good for seasons to come.

STEP 1

Protect the workspace. Spread a towel or newspaper on your work surface. Shoe polish can be messy and difficult to remove from fabrics.

149

STEP 2

Clean the footwear. Use a brush and damp cloth to remove any dirt from the shoes/boots. Be sure to allow shoes/boots to completely dry before applying any shoe polish.

STEP 3

Apply polish. If using liquid polish, glide the polish with the applicator in small circular motions over the entire shoe/boot. If using wax polish, use the cloth applicator that is usually supplied with the polish. The shoe/boot will look cloudy.

STEP 4

Let shoe dry. Wait 15–20 minutes to allow shoe polish to dry.

STEP 5

Get to shining. Use the shine brush over the entire shoe/boot. Be sure not to neglect the sides or back of the shoe/boot. Quick, side-to-side strokes ensure maximum shine.

STEP 6

Buff. Using a soft cloth, buff your shoes/boots with a side-to-side motion until they shine. Make sure to buff the sides, using the same back-and-forth motion to ensure they have a uniform shine.

STEP 7

Clean up. Put all of your shoeshine supplies together for next time and clean up your workspace.

More Info

If your leather shoes or boots have laces, remove the shoelaces every few shines. This allows you to get the shoes' tongues clean and polished to match the shine. If you wear stylish colored laces, remove them for each shining and don't re-lace before checking each eyelet for polish residue.

Wear a Scarf

YOU WILL NEED:	TIME REQUIRED:
• Scarf	30–60 seconds
• Mirror	

O f all the fun accessories in your closet, the scarf is easily the most versatile. From simple patterns to detailed weaves, scarves look good however you decide to tie, tuck, or drape. You can add pizzazz to your wardrobe/outfit by wearing this single piece of fabric—whether it's square, rectangular, or infinity—dozens of different ways.

STEP **1**

Choose the scarf. Scarves are intended to be worn around your neck and close to your face, so choose a fabric that feels good and complements

either your outfit or outerwear for the day. If worn well, your outfit will be both comfortable and coordinated.

Wrap it right. Spend the time needed to twist, drape, knot, and tuck your scarf to look just the way you want. Three popular wrap styles are "The Double Loop 'Infinity,'" "The Loop," and "The European." These styles are shown with directions in the illustrations of this chapter. Follow the directions according to the look you desire.

Own it, girl! Wear it well and with confidence to the beach or a wedding, out on a date, or to school—the choice is yours.

Fact or Fiction:

Silk is stronger than steel.

Fact. It's true. A silkworm produces one of the strongest natural fibers known to man. The pound-for-pound tensile strength of silk is greater than industrial steel. Silkworm cocoons are made of a single continuous thread of raw silk around 1 kilometer (⅔ of a mile) long. That makes for one strong chrysalis.

Sew On a Button

YOU WILL NEED:
- Button
- Thread
- Sewing needle
- Scissors

TIME REQUIRED:
5–10 minutes

*B*uttons were originally sewed to clothes as an ornamental fashion statement. It wasn't until the invention of the buttonhole in the thirteenth century that the little round objects gained the functional value we still use today. Traditionally, women's clothing buttons right over left. Why the opposite of men's buttons? Well, everybody has an opinion, but the truth is . . . nobody really knows.

STEP **1**

Thread the needle. Push one end of the thread through the eye of the needle. Pull about 12 inches of thread through the eye. Cut the

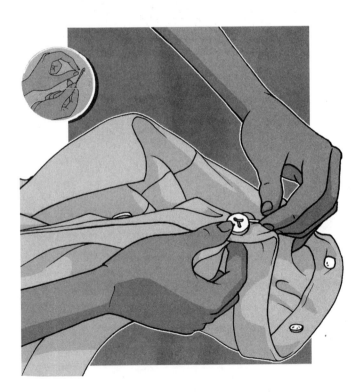

thread off the spool an equal 12 inches from the needle and tie the two ends together in a knot.

STEP **2**

Position the button. Place the button in line with other buttons and directly opposite the buttonhole.

STEP **3**

Begin sewing. From the underside of the cloth, push the threaded needle up and through the cloth and one of the button's holes.

Pull the thread through until you reach the knot. For buttons with two holes, push the threaded needle back down through the other hole, then continue sewing with the needle coming up from underneath the first hole and down through the second. Do this 6 to 8 times until the button is securely in place. If the button has four holes, sew through the holes in a way that creates an X thread pattern on the front of the button.

STEP **4**

Create the shank. On the last stitch, push the needle up from the underside of the garment, but not through the button's holes. Wind the thread around the threads at the base of the button several times to reinforce the shank. Push the needle back down through the fabric. Leaving plenty of thread for the next step, cut the needle free.

STEP **5**

Tie and trim. Tie a knot with the two ends of the thread, close to the fabric. Once the knot is secure, trim the excess thread ends with scissors.

Did You Know?

Until the nineteenth century, most buttons were used for men's clothing. Hooks and lacing were the norm for women's clothes. It wasn't until the mid-1800s that women became the primary consumers of buttons.

Spot Treat a Stain

YOU WILL NEED:

- Cold water
- Paper towel
- Spoon or dull knife
- Treatment solution—detergent, vinegar, lemon juice
- Washing machine or professional dry cleaner

TIME REQUIRED:

30 minutes

You decided to wear your favorite white shirt to dinner and your little brother managed to side-squirt you with the ketchup. Of course! Don't worry, it might be a mess, but you can probably get this stain out. Follow these simple steps and your white shirt may make a public appearance again!

STEP 1

Identify the staining substance. Different stains require different treatments. If it is ketchup or another thick substance, first use a spoon or dull knife to scrape off any excess without spreading it or forcing it farther into the fabric.

STEP 2

Soak the stain. Immediately wetting the stain with cold water is a safe first step in preventing the stain from setting into the fabric. Wetting the stain from the back of the fabric can be helpful.

STEP 3

Select treatment solution. Based on the staining substance, pick your treatment. Mild acids like vinegar or lemon juice will fight coffee or tea, while laundry or dish detergent works best on ketchup, grease, blood, chocolate, lipstick, or makeup.

STEP 4

Lightly apply treatment solution. From the back of the fabric, lightly dab the proper solution to the stain to drive the stain back to the surface.

Do not apply directly down onto the stained area as this may push the stain deeper into the fabric.

STEP 5

Lay stain facedown. Set the stained fabric facedown on a paper towel. This gives the staining substance something to escape into.

STEP 6

Give it a rest. Time is your friend, so let the treatment work on the stain. But do not allow the material to dry, as this could set the stain and possibly make it even bigger.

STEP 7

Rinse away. After 15–30 minutes, rinse the stained area under cool water to hopefully wash away both the solution and the stain. If the stain isn't fully gone, try some lemon water or vinegar to remove more of the stain and rinse again after 15–20 minutes.

STEP **8**

Wash away. If possible, immediately launder the fabric or take it to a professional dry cleaner.

More Info

Never use an acid-based, bleach, or chlorine stain treatment on wool fabrics.

Fold a Shirt

YOU WILL NEED:
- Short- or long-sleeved shirt

TIME REQUIRED:
1 minute

Clean and organized rooms and closets look good and make it easy to find an outfit, especially if you are in a hurry. Take a minute while your clothes are clean and put them where they belong. Even if that means folding a few shirts, you will be glad you did it now rather than finding that the shirt is full of wrinkles when you want to wear it.

STEP **1**

Button up. If the shirt has buttons, button the shirt all the way up.

STEP **2**

Flip it over. Lay your shirt facedown on a clean, flat work surface.

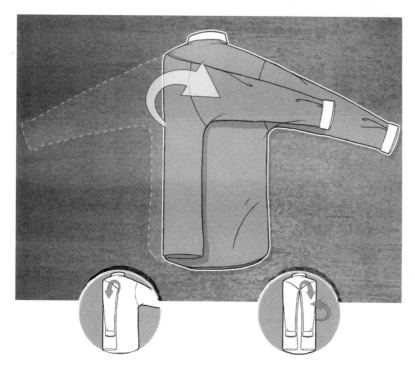

Smooth it out. Run your hands across your shirt to smooth all wrinkles or bunches.

STEP 4

Start on the right. Create a vertical fold inward from the point halfway down the shoulder to the bottom of the shirt.

STEP 5

Fold the sleeve. Fold the sleeve forward so that it lines up with the edge of the vertical fold. This will create an angled fold on the shoulder.

STEP 6

Repeat. Repeat STEP 5 with the other side.

STEP 7

Fold the bottom. Take bottom 6 inches of the shirt and fold it upward.

STEP 8

Match it up. Divide the remaining body of the shirt in half and fold it up to meet the top of the shirt.

STEP 9

Flip it over. Turn the shirt over so that it is facing right side up.

Wise Woman

"Fashion fades, only style remains the same."[4]

—Coco Chanel, French fashion designer and businesswoman

Shop for a Bra

YOU WILL NEED:
· cloth tape measure

TIME REQUIRED:
5 minutes

Some people love it, some hate it. Shopping for bras takes time and can be expensive, yet finding the right fit is important to how you feel. Few annoyances can frustrate like when a bra's underwire pokes, a strap pulls, or when nothing seems to fit right.

For young girls, starting out with a training-type bra, camisole, or sports bra may be the way to go. When it's time to find a more supportive bra, you will need to measure yourself or ask to be fitted at an undergarment retail store to find your correct bra size. There are two measurements and three steps to be properly fitted for a bra and, from there, multiple style options within your size. You may need to try on many bras to find a fit that works best for you. Use the simple measuring guide below.

Measure your bust. Place the measuring tape around the largest part of your bust. No exhale required.

Measure around your rib cage (for the band size). Make the same type of measurement just under your bust, all the way around your rib cage where the bra band will be. This should make a pretty straight line around your rib cage. Exhale and take a measurement, rounding to the nearest whole number. If it's an odd number, move up to the next even number for your band size.

Find your cup size. Subtract your band measurement from your bust measurement and that number will correlate to your cup size. The chart below shows how your number correlates to your letter cup size.

Bust Minus Band	US Cup Size	European	UK
Less than 1"	AA	AA	AA
1"	A	A	A
2"	B	B	B
3"	C	C	C
4"	D	D	D
5"	DD/E	E	DD

More Info

T-shirt test: Try on a T-shirt over a bra you like before you decide to buy it. Sometimes a bra that fits well and feels good doesn't look so good under your clothes.

7

Sports & Recreation

Sports and recreation provide a place to connect with others, make new friends, experience the power of team, travel, and ultimately enjoy the benefits of a healthy lifestyle. It isn't important that you are the best at something, but that you are trying your best and are enjoying yourself and your community.

—MEGAN MANTHEY RICHEY

You don't have to be a super-athlete with mad skills to enjoy playing the game, yet when your nickname growing up was exactly that, "Skills," it's no surprise when a girl goes pro. Former professional soccer/football player Megan Manthey Richey knows a thing or two about living an active life both on and off the field.

From as early as four years old, Megan knew she wanted to be an athlete. She took to the field a year earlier than her friends and dominated from the start. She first played on her brother's all-boys team—except for Megan that is. "I was told I could hold my own and it was probably playing with all the boys that gave me a little extra competitiveness," she recalls.[1] Her competitive drive scored her points in other sports too. Soccer was not her only game; basketball, gymnastics, and horseback riding rounded Megan out as an all-season athlete. But it was soccer, the planet's most popular sport (called *football* worldwide), that captured the favor of the girl who aspired to hear "GOOOOAAAALLLL" cheered by her team's adoring fans.

Megan knew that before she could ever score a game-winning goal as a professional she'd have to set goals for herself and work hard to accomplish them. "I put in endless hours of training both with my teams and on my own. I thought a lot about the saying, 'It matters what you do when nobody is watching,' which drove me to compete with myself to get quicker, stronger, and faster by beating my own records. Knowing I wanted to become a professional one day helped me stick to my practice schedule. I knew I needed to outwork anyone else with the same dream in order to make it all happen."

Well, dreams do come true, for the dedicated. Megan played in high school, on select teams, and in college, and eventually the big league called. In Europe she played pro on teams in Denmark, France, and Iceland. The Boston Breakers and Seattle Sounders brought Megan's career back to the States. But there is so much more to Megan than her love for competition. Relationships matter most to her. "The game allowed me to travel the world and instantly find connections with countless people. The friendships I formed all over the world are a result of sharing a common love for the game."

Megan is no longer circling the globe as a professional player. She says, "Becoming a professional athlete was really cool, and I am so glad that's a part of my story. What I've really learned about leading a healthy, active life as a young woman is important and sets a girl up for a healthy adulthood." Now officially retired, she has added wife, mom, and businesswoman to her most treasured titles. As an entrepreneur, she founded a training center to work with student athletes, teaching them how to become their best selves not only physically but spiritually, emotionally, and relationally. "I have realized a new dream. To impact the lives of as many young female athletes as possible and it's the BEST job ever!" Megan is quick to share, "Everything I have done up to this point in my life has led me directly to what I am doing now. All of the bad coaches, the best coaches, the winning teams, the failing teams, the injuries, and all the lessons learned along the way started shaping the vision I had for my business and how I could help girls transform into incredible women."

Soccer, football, swimming, running, rowing, dancing . . . there are so many options for you to be active. Don't let inactivity limit your future. Find something that works for you. Some physical activity you like or maybe even love as much as Megan loves soccer. Keep practicing. Keep moving. Keep playing. Play on!

Kick a Soccer Ball

YOU WILL NEED:
· Soccer ball
· Open space

TIME REQUIRED:
Lots of practice

*T*he argument rages between Europeans and Americans about the proper name of this game. Originally a British game called *soccer*, the competitive act of striking a ball forward into a goal has roots dating back through Chinese history to the third century BC. On October 26, 1863, English team officials met to establish a standard set of rules to be played in all matches of the game they termed *football*. Today the most popular team sport played in the world is the "other" football, with the exception of the US where American football ranks #1. What the rest of the world calls *football* is known as *soccer* in the USA—just like it was before 1863 by high-browed Brits in England. There, that should settle the argument. Or not.

Warm up. Get your legs warmed up and stretched out before exercise. This will increase your performance and reduce potential injuries.

Drop the ball. With plenty of space in front of you, drop the ball on the ground.

Step back. Take a few steps back from the ball. You don't need a running start, so don't even think about sprinting at the ball from fifteen paces.

Pick your planter foot. Your *planter* is the foot you'll plant next to the ball while kicking. It's not the one you are going to kick the ball with.

Approach the ball. From two paces back, step toward the ball straight on.

Place your planter foot. When you arrive at the ball, plant your non-kicking foot in a direct line beside the ball. Too far back and you will strike the ball low. Too far forward and you'll strike high.

Point your planter foot. The direction you point your planter foot is the direction you want the kicked ball to travel.

Swing your leg. Bring your kicking leg back to generate some striking speed. In a single motion, rotate your hips and swing your leg forward. Knee straight to pass the ball. Knee bent to shoot.

Strike the ball. With your ankle locked, strike the ball with your kicking foot. Contact the ball halfway up the laces of your foot for a power kick or on the inside to direct or pass.

Keep your balance. Use your arms to balance yourself while kicking. You'll look a bit like a scarecrow at first. So keep practicing.

Wise Woman

"What I love most about soccer are the lessons learned about discipline, hard work, overcoming failure, and teamwork."[2]

—Megan Manthey Richey, professional soccer player, Boston Breakers, Seattle Sounders

Set a Volleyball

YOU WILL NEED:
- Volleyball
- Teammates (although you can practice alone)

TIME REQUIRED:
Lots of practice

*B*ump, SET, spike! Game point! Fun to do, difficult to execute. Volleyball is a game of measured attacks that often hinge on a skillfully set ball to be powerfully spiked over the net. This means setting a volleyball properly is all about consistency and quality. Master the overhead set and your teammates will thrive on your ability to place the ball just where they need to hard-drive it home.

STEP 1

Warm up. Get your body warmed up and stretch out your legs and arms before exercise. This will increase your performance and reduce potential injuries.

STEP 2

Get to the ball. Seldom will the ball come to you, so get moving to the ball. Make your move quick and efficient. Take as few steps as needed.

STEP 3

Square up. When you get in position with the ball, square your shoulders, hips, and feet in the direction the ball is approaching.

STEP 4

Get your hands up. Extend your arms over your head with a slight outward bend in your elbows. Keep your hands about 6 inches directly above your forehead. Spread your fingers wide in the shape of the ball, like the ball is about to rest in your hands. Your thumbs and fingers

should form a triangular window through which you can see the ball. Your hands should not actually touch each another.

Position your feet. Spread your feet to be about shoulder-width apart, with your foot closest to the net slightly in front of the other.

Bend your knees. Before making contact with the ball, bend your knees slightly and distribute your weight evenly between the balls of your feet and arches.

Set the ball. When your hands contacts the ball, it should occur just above the center of your forehead. As soon as the ball touches your fingers, straighten your arms and legs at the same time, pushing the ball upward in the direction you choose.

Follow through. At the end of your set, both arms should be fully extended and your hands straightened at the wrist in the direction of the ball's release.

More Info

10 Basic Volleyball Terms

ace: A serve that is not passable and results immediately in a point.

block: When a player jumps at the net with her extended arms to stop a spike from the other team.

dig: When a player bounces the ball into the air using both hands.

dink: A legal push of the ball around or over blockers.

double hit: Successive hits or contacts by the same player (illegal).

rotation: The clockwise movement of players around the court and through the serving position following a side out.

serve: Used to put the ball into play.

set: The tactical skill in which a ball is directed to a point where a player can spike it into the opponent's court.

spike: A hard smash of the ball over the net.

wipe: When a hitter pushes the ball off the opposing block so it lands out of bounds.

Throw a Football

YOU WILL NEED:
- American football
- Throwing partner

TIME REQUIRED:
Lots of practice

*T*here may not be many female football leagues around, but that doesn't mean you can't throw a football! Passing the pigskin around with friends or knowing how to throw when that Thanksgiving Day flag football game gets going is fun! Get good enough and your dreams of a college scholarship could come true, as certain schools are starting to offer girls signings in their football programs. Down, set, HIKE!

STEP **1**

Warm up. Get your throwing arm warmed up and stretched out before exercise. This will increase your accuracy and reduce potential injury.

Get a grip. Hold the football toward the back of the laces. Two or three fingers should grip the laces while your thumb wraps around the other side of the ball. Your thumb and index finger should form the letter **L**. Hold the football with your fingertips just enough that your palm is slightly raised off the surface of the ball.

Assume the position. The stance of your feet is important to throwing a football. Move your feet so your body is positioned at a 90-degree angle relative to your target—if you're right-handed, turn to your right, with your left foot forward. Pivot your front foot to point in the direction of your throw and keep your eyes on the potential target.

Ready your throw. Bend your throwing arm into a position that holds the ball comfortably just above your throwing shoulder and below your ear. You can steady the ball with your opposite hand if needed. Now your arm is ready to throw the ball forward in a circular arc.

Throw the ball. In a single motion, drop the ball back a bit behind your shoulder, then move your arm forward in a circular arc while extending your elbow. At the same time, step forward on your front foot and pivot your upper body in the direction of your target. As you release the ball, it should roll off your fingertips, with the index finger last off the ball, which gives it a spiral. Snap your wrist at the release. This coordinated motion in your arm, body, and feet gives the throw direction and power.

Did You Know?

Becca Longo is the first female to receive a college scholarship at a Division I or II university for football. Becca received the scholarship from Adams State University in Colorado as a kicker, the same position she played on her high school football team.

Shoot a Basketball

YOU WILL NEED:
· Basketball
· Hoop

TIME REQUIRED:
Lots of practice

Warm up. Get your body warmed up and stretch out your legs and arms before exercise. This will increase your performance and reduce potential injuries.

Take a stand. Balance yourself with your feet shoulder width apart. Face the basket with your dominant foot a half step in front of your

other foot. Bend your knees slightly while keeping your back straight and shoulders facing the hoop.

STEP **3**

Get a grip. Spread your fingers and cradle the ball from below in your shooting hand while steadying the ball from the side with your other hand. The basketball should rest on your finger-tips, leaving a shallow pocket between the ball and the palm of your hand. Ready the ball for a shot by holding it in the space between your chest and chin.

> **Basketball**
> Boys invented it . . .
> Girls perfected it.

STEP **4**

Take the shot. Facing the hoop and in a coordinated motion, straighten your knees and push upward as you raise the ball from the ready position, up in front of your face, while extending your arms upward and forward. Do not bring the ball back to a position near your ear.

STEP **5**

Release the ball. When you reach your full shot extension, release the ball by rolling the shot off the tips of your shooting hand's index and middle fingers. As the ball leaves your hand, snap your wrist so the shot follows an arched path toward the basket. No line drives allowed.

STEP **6**

Follow through. Keep your shot form until the ball hits the rim. Don't jump forward or fade backward like some overly confident street ball wannabe. Your feet should land in the same position from where you started the shot.

Did You Know?

Invented in 1891, the game of basketball got its start with players dribbling a soccer ball and shooting it into a peach basket hanging from a balcony.

Pitch a Softball

YOU WILL NEED:
- Softball
- Glove
- Friend to play catcher

TIME REQUIRED:
Lots of practice

Zara Mee set a Guinness Book world record when she sent a softball screaming 68.9 mph (111 km/h) over home plate. Consider the level of difficulty facing her batters. Swing a round bat in an attempt to hit a round ball—squarely. And at highway-fast speeds. That's no easy task. STRIKE! Bringing that kind of heat requires strength, accuracy, and lots of practice. Learn to throw a fast-pitch softball and you will be a hit with more coaches than batters.

STEP 1

The warm-up. Get your body warmed up and stretch out your arms, shoulder, and legs before exercise. This will increase your performance and reduce potential injuries.

STEP 2

The grip. Grip the softball with your fingers spread across the "C" shape of the stitched seam and your thumb on the opposite side of the ball.

STEP 3

The stance. Stand with your push-off foot—right for righties, left for lefties—on the front of the pitching rubber. Your other foot rests behind you, on or against the rubber, and your hips are square to the catcher.

STEP 4

The rotation. This is an underhand pitch, so swing your pitching hand down past your hip, up to shoulder level behind you. Then bring it back down and around, whipping your arm around like a windmill and taking a long stride forward with your back foot.

STEP **5**

The release. When the forward swing of your pitching arm reaches your thigh, release the ball with a flick of your wrist.

STEP **6**

The follow-through. Let your arm finish the swing all the way through.

Did You Know?

The human body's ability to "bring the heat" may hit its limit at 100 miles per hour. Why, you ask? The amount of torque required to toss at these speeds exceeds the amount of force the elbow ligament can withstand before experiencing damage.

Swing a Golf Club

YOU WILL NEED:	TIME REQUIRED:
· Golf club	Lots of practice
· Golf ball	
· Golf tee	

STEP 1

Get a grip. If you're right-handed, grasp the club with your left hand. (Reverse for lefties.) Grip the club with your right hand below your left. Move your right hand's pinky finger to sit between the left hand's index and middle fingers. Your left thumb should set into the palm of your right hand.

STEP 2

Take a stand. With your feet shoulder width apart, stand bent forward from the hips with your back in a straight, neutral position.

Address the ball. Stand a comfortable distance from the ball. Close enough that your club's face meets the ball flush, yet far enough back to not crowd your swing. Your arms should be straight.

STEP **4**

Backswing. As you swing back, keep your lead arm straight yet allow your other arm to bend slightly. Rotate your upper body as you raise your club to create a 90-degree angle between your lead forearm and the club. Your head should remain motionless, looking down at the ball.

STEP **5**

Forward swing. Swing your arms down, drawing the club forward in a circular motion. The club's head should lag behind the forearms at 90 degrees yet rapidly unwind to be in near straight alignment with the arms at the point of impact.

STEP **6**

Follow through. Past the point of impact with the ball, continue to swing the club around, up, and over your shoulder. A correct follow-through will position your body with your belt buckle facing the target, club behind you, and your back foot balanced on its toe.

Fact or Fiction:

Shooting a hole in one is an individual's call— all a golfer needs to do is keep the ball and have her scorecard signed by the club pro.

Fiction. The fact is, for a hole in one to be "official," the golfer must be playing at least a nine-hole round, play only one ball during the round, and another person must witness the shot.

Putt

YOU WILL NEED:
- Golf club (putter)
- Golf ball

TIME REQUIRED:
Lots of practice

*W*hether it's a putt for the win at a game of golf or a putt for the win at Putt-Putt mini golf, knowing how to gently tap that little golf ball into a little hole is fun and frustrating! The greens on a well-manicured golf course are a lot different from the AstroTurf of mini golf, but practice can be done regardless. There are golf lessons offered by golf pros around the country, and if you're really into the game, they may be well worth the money. The following steps will get you started and on your way to a mini golf win!

STEP **1**

Get a grip. For righties, grasp the putter with your left hand (reverse the instructions for lefties). Grip the club with your right hand below

your left. Move your right hand's pinky finger to sit between your left hand's index and middle fingers. Your left thumb should set into the palm of your right hand.

STEP **2**

Take a stand. With your feet shoulder width apart, put a little flex in your knees. Draw in your elbows snug to your ribs and tilt your upper body forward. This should allow you to comfortably and gently rest the club's head behind the ball.

STEP **3**

Address the ball. Resting the putter just behind the ball, step toward the ball until your toes stand about 2½ putter-head lengths from the near side of the ball. Lean forward slightly and position your body centerline to the ball.

STEP **4**

Make the stroke. Ready, aim, stroke. Don't think too hard. Just make a smooth, flowing stroke with the putter toward the cup. One and done.

More Info

An expensive putter can cost upwards of several hundred dollars. A bargain bin putter will put you in the hole only a couple of bucks at your neighborhood yard sale. Neither will make you a better golfer. A keen eye and lots of practice are what pay in the end.

Throw Darts

YOU WILL NEED:	TIME REQUIRED:
• Set of darts	Lots of practice
• Dartboard	

*I*s this a game of darts or a lesson in mechanical science? A bit of both, actually. Physics controls levers, hinges, joints, acceleration, parabolic curves, deceleration, and your emotions. Emotions? Well, yes, if you get excited about hitting the bull's-eye in a game of darts! You used levers, hinges, joints, acceleration, parabolic curves, and deceleration to strike the very center of the board. Good thing is, you needn't have a math addiction to master the game, yet possessing a healthy respect for the laws of physics does help.

STEP 1

Get a grip. Find the dart's center balancing point. Grasp the dart a bit behind the center of gravity with your thumb and your preference of one or two fingers.

Take aim. Think of your eyes, the dart, and the target all needing to line up. Focus on the exact spot on the board you want to hit. This is your target. Don't let anybody walking by distract you.

Power up. Bend your arm at the elbow and slowly draw your forearm back toward your face. Most accurate throwers stop just shy of the chin or beside the cheek. Avoid direct dart-to-eye contact.

Accelerate. Hinging at the elbow, smoothly accelerate your forearm toward the target. Don't go too fast, you'll lose control. Don't go too slow, you'll lose a toe.

Release. Think naturally. When your arm, wrist, and dart reach the forward-most acceleration point, let the dart fly at the target you haven't taken your eye off of since you got a grip. Raise your elbow and the dart will overshoot the target. Hang on too long and the dart will land too low.

Follow through. Your hand should complete the throw pointing at the target. Not only will this grant you greater accuracy, but you can also point at your shot and proclaim, "Sweet! Did you see that?"

Did You Know?

Due to danger of impalement, lawn darts have been banned in the United States since 1988 and in Canada since 1989.

Hit a Cue Ball

YOU WILL NEED:
- Pool table
- Straight pool cue
- Pool balls

TIME REQUIRED:
Lots of practice

Billiards—General name for cue game sports played on a felt-covered, railed table. The most popular in the world are pool and snooker.

Pool—The family of cue game sports played on a pool table with six rail pockets. One white cue ball is used to strike a combination of up to 15 solid and striped balls into the rail pockets.

Snooker—A cue game sport played on a table that holds six rail pockets and measures 12 ft. x 6 ft. Snooker is played with 22 balls—1 white cue ball, 15 red balls, and 6 additional balls that are each a different color, including yellow, green, brown, blue, pink, and black.

Set your bridge. Set your nondominant hand on the table in front of the cue ball. Slide your thumb up against the side of your index finger into a V shape. This is the bridge and guide for the cue stick.

Take aim. Hold the cue stick at the wide end with your dominant hand and set the narrowing end into the V shape of your bridge hand. Keeping the stick level, slowly draw the cue stick back and forth a few times to practice aiming straight at the exact spot on the cue ball you want to strike.

Practice hit. On an open table, practice hitting the cue ball in a straight line from one end of the table, off the opposite cushion, and directly back to you.

Practice strike. Place one billiard ball ahead of the cue ball and practice hitting the cue ball in a straight line into the other billiard ball. Try aiming the cue ball's strike so the billiard ball ricochets off and into a side or corner pocket.

Play the game. With practice and an eye for angles, your game will improve.

More Info

"Never set the pool cue chalk, chalk side down. The blue dust will get all over the rail, your clothes, hands, and you just know that your nose only itches when you have blue fingers."

—Roger Stensland, billiards player (Jonathan's grandfather)

Pitch Horseshoes

YOU WILL NEED:
- Horseshoe set
- Two 14-inch-tall stakes in the ground, 40 feet apart

TIME REQUIRED:
Lots of practice

Sitting around at a picnic or other outdoor event is not the place to stare into your phone. Look up, keep your phone put away, and get to know people around you. If there's a game of horseshoes going, get involved. All you need to do is pick up a horseshoe, make sure no one is standing in your way, and toss it toward the stake in the other horseshoe pit. If you totally miss, no problem! Laugh about it—that is half the fun! Or maybe you'll get really good and the competition will no longer be about just "horsing around"!

Grip to flip. Hold the horseshoe in your pitching hand. There is no rule about how you must grip the 2½-pound horseshoe. The grip that flips the horseshoe when tossed is thumb on top and fingers beneath, slightly off-center of the middle of the shoe.

Stand behind the foul line. To one side of the pit and stake, stand with feet together in preparation to toss.

Step forward. Holding the horseshoe in your pitching hand, extend your pitching arm and swing it underhand and back alongside your body. At the same time, gain balance and throwing rhythm by stepping forward with the leg opposite your throwing arm. So long as your foot does not cross the foul line (which measures 27 or 37 feet from the opposite target stake), step as you please.

Pitch the shoe. As you step forward, underhand swing your pitching arm back and then forward alongside your body. When your pitching arm, hand, and horseshoe all align with your target stake, release or "pitch" the shoe.

Follow through. Let your pitching arm remain raised as the horseshoe flips through the air toward the opposite pit and stake.

Fact or Fiction:

Pitching horseshoes is all about power.

Fiction. The fact is, each horseshoe only weighs 2½ pounds. This game is all about aim and strategy.

8

Cars & Driving

You don't have to sit around and play with dolls if you want to play with cars or build something with your hands.[1]

—ALLISON BORMANN,
BMW driving instructor

*D*riven to succeed. Perhaps there is no better way to describe a woman whose driving history includes wins with NASCAR,[2] NASA,[3] and SCCA[4] racing. The auto racing record books held her name in 2000 as the highest overall finishing female in the Daytona 24-hour race. She was the first NASCAR Drive for Diversity driver to win a race and the first female ever to win a NASCAR Late Model Stock Car race at Stockton Speedway. There's not a drift track, skid pad, or hot lap that intimidates her. So it should come as no surprise to learn she has also steered her career into the elite position of a BMW Performance Driving School instructor.

Meet Allison Bormann, mechanical engineer, gearhead, and professional driver. Her road-racing résumé includes everything from NASCAR's checkered flag wins to Hollywood's red-carpet events, big time sponsorships to teen driver training volunteer. Revved and ready to go since she was a little girl, Allison grew up riding shotgun in her father's passion for the sport of auto racing. A professional driver on two continents, her dad liked watching the races trackside almost as much as he loved being behind the wheel. At age six, Allison stood by her dad to watch her first live NASCAR race. "I thought it was the coolest thing I had ever seen. Yes, I was that little kid hanging on the fence, staring, watching, cheering as the cars went by. I was immediately hooked!" Good thing Allison's dad also owned an auto repair shop specializing in British sports cars. "We got a couple of little street cars and turned them into race cars and when I was old enough to drive, I started racing." Like father, like daughter . . . once Allison took hold of the wheel there was no looking back.

Despite all her raw horsepower, Allison didn't merge straight into the fast lane of racing. After high school, she followed the inspiration of her favorite professional driver and attended college in pursuit of a mechanical engineering degree. In addition to her studies, she spent almost every weekend on the track, chasing the checkered flag. Winning races was her thing in college, and with each lap Allison paid her dues and moved way up in the rankings. Following graduation, she turned down multiple opportunities, including an offer to race in Europe, to follow her dreams by moving to the heart of NASCAR country—Charlotte, North Carolina.

Now a few years and countless miles later, the once-aspiring driver is a seasoned pro. Allison's lifetime of behind-the-wheel experience has earned her a position worth following. Luxury sports car drivers from around the world heed her instructions about what matters most when it comes to proper acceleration, braking, turns, and paying attention to the road both on the track and through city streets. "The two most important things in driving are to limit your distractions and to look ahead as far as you can," Allison tells all her students.

> Limit distractions. "So many accidents today are caused by people who are distracted and not paying attention." This means no cell phones, messages, or posts while driving.
>
> Look ahead as far as you can. "Most people are not looking far enough ahead to give themselves enough time to react and respond to what's going on in front of them. Maybe there's a car slamming on its brakes or there's a corner ahead they'll need to slow down for before entering." So, look up and look ahead.

Allison believes these two simple yet significant principles are also good habits to follow while navigating life. "Some people like to wing it, but that's not a very successful or safe way to make it down the road."

Allison also knows that girls today can pave their own way ahead. "You don't have to sit around and play with dolls if you want to play with cars, build with your hands, or get into technology-based industries." Basically, Allison wants to inspire girls to drive toward any destination they choose in life and on the road. "Just remember, all driving is a very serious matter. It's something that requires a lot of attention and focus. Driving is a privilege and not a right. It's one of the most dangerous things many people will ever do. If you don't take it seriously, it can be taken away. It's that important."[5]

Shift a Manual Transmission

YOU WILL NEED:
- Vehicle with a manually shifting transmission
- Empty parking lot or level road without traffic

TIME REQUIRED:
30 minutes, plus lots of practice

*F*ewer and fewer vehicles are made with manual transmissions (aka *stick shift*). That doesn't mean you shouldn't know how to drive one. When you begin driving, see if you can find a manual transmission and someone who will let you give it a go. Knowing how to drive a manual transmission can be really fun!

STEP **1**

Sit safe. Adjust the seat so your body is a comfortable distance from the steering wheel and pedals. Both your knees and elbows should remain

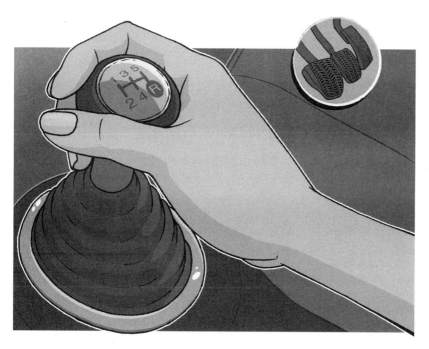

slightly bent. The parking brake should be set. (There is no Park in a manual transmission, so the parking brake is what keeps your car from rolling.)

STEP **2**

Press the clutch and brake pedals down. Notice there are three pedals. From left to right—clutch, brake, and gas (accelerator). With your left foot on the clutch and your right foot on the brake, push both pedals all the way to the floor and hold them there.

STEP **3**

Shift into neutral. Use your right hand to move the gearshift into neutral, the center position between the gears where the gearshift will move from side to side with ease.

STEP **4**

Start the engine. With the clutch and brake still depressed, turn the key to start the car. Release the handbrake.

STEP **5**

Shift into first gear. With your right hand, shift the car into "1" (first) gear.

STEP **6**

Release the brake. Lift your right foot off the brake pedal and place it on the accelerator (far right pedal).

STEP **7**

Release the clutch while giving it some gas. Smoothly lift your left foot, releasing the clutch pedal from the floor. As you release the clutch with your left foot, SLOWLY accelerate. If you release the clutch too quickly, the vehicle will lurch forward and stall. Coordinating the gas and clutch is key to moving forward and will keep the engine from stalling or revving. With practice, you will find the catch point where the clutch engages smoothly.

Shift up. When the RPMs exceed 3,000, shift up to a higher gear. Lift your right foot off the gas, push in the clutch with your left, shift to the next higher gear, lift the clutch, and give it gas again to accelerate.

Shift down. When the RPMs drop below 2,500, shift down to a lower gear. Lift your right foot off the gas, push in the clutch with your left, shift to a lower gear, and lift the clutch.

Stop. As the car slows, shift down one gear at a time and, just prior to stopping, shift into neutral or hold in the clutch pedal to disengage the transmission, braking with your right foot.

More Info

DO NOT over-recline the driver's seat. Safely controlling the steering wheel, brake, clutch, and gas pedals is far more important than how you look while driving. Besides, foolish is how you'll look after crashing your car because of a lack of control.

Change a Flat Tire

YOU WILL NEED:
- Spare tire
- Jack
- Lug nut wrench (usually incorporated into the jack handle)

TIME REQUIRED:
15–30 minutes

*D*id you know that many newer model cars no longer come equipped with a spare tire? New car or not, do you know if your car has a spare? If it doesn't, you'll want to know how roadside service works and how to brace yourself for the cost of a tow and tire change. If your car does have a spare, save your time and money by learning to change a tire yourself, and you'll soon be back on the road again.

Gather your tools. Locate and remove from your car the spare tire, jack, and lug nut wrench. Position each beside the car close to where you will be changing the flat tire.

IMPORTANT

When preparing to change a flat tire, always have the car's gearshift lever in Park and set the parking brake. If the car has a manual transmission, shift into 1st (first) gear and set the parking brake.

STEP **2**

Loosen the lug nuts. Before raising the car, use the flat end of the lug nut wrench to pry free the hubcap (if necessary) and the socket end to loosen the lug nuts. Turn each lug nut counterclockwise until only slightly loose. DO NOT completely remove the lug nuts during this step!

STEP **3**

Position the jack. Check your car's owner's manual for the correct place to position the jack under the car.

STEP **4**

Raise the car. Jack up the car to a height necessary to both remove the flat tire and install the spare. Remember the spare tire will require more clearance to install than the flat tire requires to remove.

STEP **5**

Remove the lug nuts. Finish loosening the lug nuts and place them in a safe location within arm's reach of where you are working.

STEP **6**

Remove the flat. Pull the flat tire off and roll it away from your workspace.

STEP **7**

Install the spare tire. To ensure proper placement, align the lug holes on the rim with the car's lug bolts and check to be sure the air valve faces out.

STEP **8**

Replace the lug nuts. In a crisscross star pattern, work your way around the wheel, tightening each lug nut to snug.

STEP **9**

Lower the jack. Slowly lower the jack until it's free from the weight of the car.

STEP **10**

Tighten the lug nuts. Ensure the lug nuts are fully tightened before cleaning up and driving the car.

Did You Know?

Your car could have a crush on you. NEVER place any part of your body under a car supported by a jack. If the jack gives way, you're stuck. When retrieving an object from under a jacked-up car, use something that extends your reach, like a stick, umbrella, or broom handle.

Jump-Start a Dead Battery

YOU WILL NEED:
· Jumper cables
· Another vehicle with a working battery

TIME REQUIRED:
5–10 minutes

When the car just won't start, it may be because the battery is dead. Leaving a light on in the car is one way to drain a car battery, but there are other culprits as well. Whatever the cause, using jumper cables to get the car up and running again is something every driver should know how to do. Pay attention to the IMPORTANT instructions below or the results could be shocking, to say the least.

STEP **1**

Find the jumper cables. It's always a good idea to carry a pair in the trunk. If yours are "missing," ask to borrow a set.

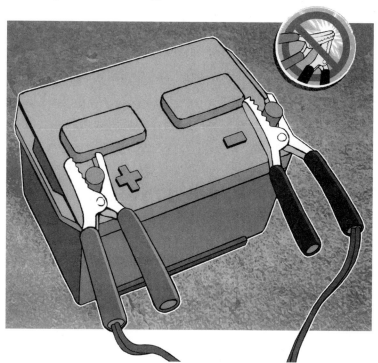

Release the hood. Pull the hood release lever. It is usually located under the dashboard between the steering wheel and the driver's door.

Open the hood. Reach under the front of the hood to locate the hood latch. Pull it and lift the hood open. If needed, secure it open with the safety arm that either extends up to the hood or down from the hood.

Position the second vehicle. Park the second vehicle next to your car close enough that the jumper cables will reach between the two cars' batteries.

IMPORTANT

Be sure to turn the second car OFF before connecting the jumper cables.

Connect the red clamps. First, connect one red positive (+) clamp to the dead battery's positive (+) terminal. Second, connect the other red positive (+) clamp to the good battery's positive (+) terminal.

IMPORTANT

When connecting the jumper cables, DO NOT touch the clamps to each other or any other metal on the car!

Connect the black clamps. Next, connect one black negative (-) clamp to the dead battery's negative (-) terminal. Then connect the other black negative (-) clamp to the good battery's negative (-) terminal.

Start your engines. First, start the car with the good battery and let it run for a minute or two. Second, try starting your car. If it doesn't start right away, let the battery charge for a minute before trying again.

Disconnect the cables. Once your car has started, immediately disconnect the jumper clamps from both vehicles in reverse order.

Charge it up. Keep your car running for a while before shutting it off to ensure your battery has sufficient charge.

Helpful Hint

When disconnecting the jumper cables, DO NOT touch the clamps to each other or any other metal on the car! This can cause the electrical system to short and that's expensive to fix.

Check the Oil

YOU WILL NEED:
- Shop rag or paper towel
- New engine oil
- In some cases, a flashlight

TIME REQUIRED:
5 minutes

 dipstick is the measuring device used to check the oil level in a car's engine. Today, most cars have systems that keep track of your car's oil so we don't need to check the oil manually. Still, some cars, including older and "classic" cars, require you take a look for yourself. There are also other motorized machines that use oil and have dipsticks to check oil levels, such as lawn mowers, motorcycles, generators, and more. Knowing how to check a machine's oil level can save an engine from irreversible damage.

IMPORTANT

To get an accurate reading, you will want to check the oil while the car is parked on level ground and while the engine is cool.

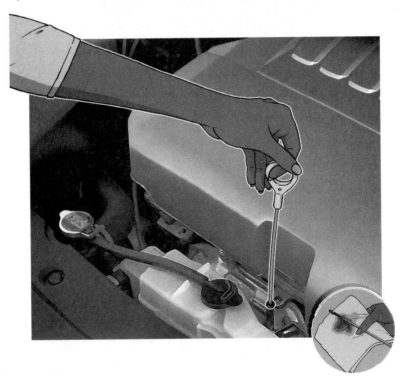

STEP 1

Release the hood. Pull the hood release lever. It is usually located under the dashboard between the steering wheel and the driver's door.

STEP 2

Open the hood. Reach under the front of the hood to locate the hood latch. Pull it and lift the hood. If needed, secure it open with the safety arm that either extends up to the hood or down from the hood.

STEP 3

Locate the dipstick. Don't confuse the engine oil dipstick with the one for the transmission fluid. Usually located near the center of the engine compartment, the oil dipstick looks like a long metal loop sticking up out of the engine. It may be a bright color and labeled "Oil."

STEP 4

Pull the dipstick. Pull the dipstick and wipe it clean, using a shop rag or paper towel.

STEP 5

Replace the cleaned dipstick. Be sure to press it down all the way. This allows the dipstick to extend fully into the engine's oil pan.

STEP 6

Pull the dipstick again. Hold it horizontally and examine the end to read the oil level. If the oil is above the top line marked "full," the oil level is too high. If the oil is below the bottom line, the oil level is too low. If the oil is between the two lines, the oil level is just right.

STEP 7

If necessary, add oil. Oil should only be added through the hole marked with the words "Engine Oil" on the cap.

STEP 8

Repeat. Follow STEPS 5 to 7 as needed until the oil level is correct. Be careful not to overfill.

Start the engine. Always replace the dipstick and "Engine Oil" cap before closing the hood or starting the engine.

Did You Know?

If the oil light is illuminated on the dashboard, this means the engine has low oil pressure, not low oil level. Continuing to run the car could severely damage the engine.

Parallel Park

YOU WILL NEED:
- Car
- Parallel parking space
- Two road cones (for practice session)
- Patience

TIME REQUIRED:
30 seconds to years

*P*arallel parking is tricky for many. People will often drive in circles and be willing to walk longer distances so they don't have to parallel park. Don't fear the parallel park—practice it! A location away from other cars and people is a good place to practice. Set up some road cones to represent the other cars you will need to avoid hitting, and keep practicing until you can glide your car into a space with no problem.

Find a space. On the same side of the street that you are driving on, find a parking space big enough for your car. Put on your right turn signal.

Line things up. Slow to a stop beside the car parked in the space ahead of where you intend to park. A good starting alignment is two to three feet between you and the other car, with the vehicles aligned side-by-side, with the rear bumpers even.

Check your mirrors. Check your side and rearview mirrors for people, obstructions, and other vehicles.

Check the street. Look over your street-side shoulder for traffic. Do not attempt to parallel park while cars try to drive around you.

Reverse your car. Shift into Reverse and back up slowly. Once the middle of your car has cleared the bumper of the parked car, turn the steering wheel all the way right and SLOWLY continue to reverse your car. Check the passenger side and front of your car as you round and pass the bumper of the other vehicle.

Straighten things out. Once your car is at a 45-degree angle to the curb, turn the wheel back to the left. This will direct the nose of your car in behind the other vehicle and bring you into parallel alignment with the parking spot.

Creep forward. Shift into Drive and CREEP your car forward. You may need to steer right to close the gap between you and the curb. Be sure to center your vehicle in the space to leave enough room for the cars in front and behind to exit their spaces.

Fact or Fiction:

Men are better parallel parkers than women.

Fiction. The fact is, it doesn't matter if the car is driven by a she or a he. What matters most is the knowledge, practice, and real-world application of mathematical angles, depth perception, and spatial relations. Yep, this is the answer to when you will actually use that boring math lesson, and math doesn't care if you are a woman or man.

Behave after an Auto Accident

YOU WILL NEED:	TIME REQUIRED:
• Car	Blink of an eye to
• License, registration & proof of insurance	crash, 1 hour plus after the crash
• Another car or ditch, wall, post . . .	

So, you've run into the bumper of the car in front of you at the stoplight. PLEASE TELL ME YOU WERE **NOT** ON YOUR CELL PHONE! Okay . . . no phone involved . . . it was an accident. This kind of thing is scary and hopefully it's nothing but a fender bender. Even better, hopefully you will never need to use this "how to"! Be safe by staying away from all distractions while driving . . . cell phones, food, makeup, or anything that will take your attention away from driving.

STEP **1**

Stay calm. Take a deep breath and remain calm. Immediately following a wreck, your adrenaline will start pumping, so focus on breathing normally to remain calm.

STEP **2**

Check for injuries. Check yourself and everybody in your car for physical injuries.

STEP **3**

Stay safe. Turn on the car's hazard lights. If possible, move your car to the side of the road, out of the flow of traffic.

STEP **4**

Call 911. Even if the crash is minor and the other person is suggesting to "take care of things personally, without cops and insurance companies," always call the police.

STEP 5

Call your insurance agent. Place a call to your insurance agent or insurance company's accident hotline. Explain your situation and listen carefully to their instructions.

STEP 6

Document everything. Take lots of pictures and notes about the accident scene, damage to vehicles or property, and all injuries.

STEP 7

Exchange information. Talk with the other driver and all witnesses. Be sure to exchange important information like names, addresses, phone numbers, insurance company information and policy numbers, driver's license numbers, and license plate numbers. Be polite, stick to the facts, and never say the accident was your fault, even if you think it was.

STEP **8**

Sign nothing. Do not sign any document unless it's for the police or YOUR insurance agent.

STEP **9**

Drive safe. If the police say your car is drivable, go only as far as needed to get your ride inspected and repaired.

More Info

Never flee from the scene of an accident. Doing so turns your accident into a hit-and-run. This results in the scene of the accident becoming the scene of the crime.

Behave during a Police Stop

YOU WILL NEED:
- Car
- Lead foot
- License, registration & proof of insurance

TIME REQUIRED:
10–20 minutes

*O*ops, a little too fast in a 35 mph zone and you're being pulled over for speeding. Keep calm, take a deep breath, and always be respectful during a police stop. It might not get you out of a ticket, but it will keep you out of additional trouble.

STEP **1**

Pull over. Put on your turn signal and look for a safe place to pull to the side of the road. Turn off your engine and wait for the officer to approach your car.

Stay in the car. Keep your seat belt fastened, turn off the music, roll down the window, and don't even think about reaching for your cell phone.

Show 'em your hands. Rest your hands on the top of the steering wheel so the approaching officer can see them both.

Provide papers. Reach for your license, vehicle registration, and proof of auto insurance only when the officer asks for them.

Answer truthfully. Look the officer in the eyes and be sure to answer their questions truthfully. No lying!

Accept it. You may or may not get a ticket. No matter what the officer decides, accept it. If you want to fight the citation, take your argument to court. Now is not the time, and the side of the road is not the place.

Fact or Fiction:

Once an officer pulls you over, they must give you a ticket.

Fiction. The fact is, "the officer will decide on what to do with you once they've had a chance to talk with you. Your truthfulness, attitude, tone of voice, and even your past driving history can influence the officer's decision to ticket or not to ticket."

—Officer B. Harris, Portland Police Department

9

Food & Cooking

This is my invariable advice to people: Learn how to cook—try new recipes, learn from your mistakes, be fearless, and above all have fun.[1]

—JULIA CHILD, American chef, author, and television personality

*D*ependent girls need someone else to feed them, while an independent woman knows her way around the kitchen. Confident and capable enough to cook for herself and certain enough to prepare food for others, a woman who can slice, dice, boil, and broil is the meal master everyone likes to be around when it's time for dinner.

Two good friends who get along great while sharing food and life are Stacey Coates and Britten Shelson. After graduating from the Culinary Institute of America in Hyde Park, New York, the women took their careers in the kitchen on the road. From Washington DC to San Francisco, New York to Maui, the ladies baked and cooked their way onto the plates and into the hearts of foodies of all ages. Stacey's career as a head pastry chef is rising fast, while Britten savors mentoring younger chefs just getting established in restaurant kitchens. Both women love the art of food and the importance of knowing how to prepare and share good meals.

With a bright smile and excitement in her voice, Britten is quick to share, "I love cooking for others because it makes people happy. Anytime I've prepared a healthy meal that someone enjoys, I feel like I'm playing a small part in their appreciation for good food. It also creates a sense of well-being and love between everyone who is sharing it. There really is something to be said for all eating together at the table."[2]

And Stacey feels much the same way. "In my travels through many kitchens, I've learned creating comes from the heart of where I am. I love things that make people happy and feel good. Gluten-free treats and chocolate chip cookies are my go-to!"[3]

So, where did their passion for preparing delicious dishes come from?

At 10 years old, Britten found her first culinary inspiration: Emeril Lagasse. One of Emeril's recipes, Helen's Sausage Bread, is still one of Britten's favorite dishes to prepare. Stacey first became interested in cooking at the age of 5 while watching her dad make crepes and pancakes every Sunday morning. Then at the age of 6, she met her first celebrity chef, Julia Child. "I was on a flight from California and I was very nervous. I kept getting up to use the bathroom and every time had to ask a tall, lovely lady if I could pass by. 'It's okay,' and the feeling of calm she shared helped me throughout the flight. I knew 13 years later that was the first lesson in my career from the great Julia Child. Walking through the front doors of the Culinary Institute of America, I experienced the same feeling of calm I'd had while sitting next to my culinary inspiration. I knew everything was going to be okay."

"When it comes to cooking, the most important thing is to not be afraid to fail, because undoubtedly you will," says Britten. "Learn from your failures and use them to move forward to be better the next time. Cooking is not hard. If you view it as a challenge comparable to climbing Mt. Everest, you will feel defeated every time. There are thousands of cookbooks out there, many with simple recipes for home cooks. Buy a book and learn something new! For yourself, your friends, and family!"

Stacey goes on to say, "Food is fuel for your body; what you put into your mouth determines how you are going to feel for the day. It plays a role in your energy levels, mood, and even clear skin! Knowing what foods are good for you and how to prepare them will set you up for a very successful, energized life!"

Cook on, my friends!

Make a Grocery List and Stock a Pantry

YOU WILL NEED:	TIME REQUIRED:
· Grocery budget	20–30 minutes
· Pen and paper	
· Meal recipes	

*H*aving a plan and knowing what you need when you go to the store can save you from overspending and from making a return trip for a forgotten item. Planning out your menu for a few days is helpful when making a grocery list, and knowing what you eat often will help you stock your pantry.

STEP 1

Know your food budget. If you go to the store without knowing how much you are able to spend, it is super easy to go way over budget. This

can cause all kinds of problems in the financial side of life, so know what you have to spend when you go to buy food.

STEP **2**

Know what you want to eat. Shopping for breakfast, lunch, and dinner? Write out what you plan to eat for the next few days. Try to stick with what you plan so that you're not wasting food, especially when planning on fresh items like veggies and meat. Find a few recipes that you like or would like to try. Make sure their ingredients aren't going to break the bank.

STEP **3**

Write your grocery list. From the meal plan and recipes you have for the next few days, write down everything you will need to purchase to make those meals. Some of the items for certain recipes may be part of your pantry list. You can find a basic pantry list below. These are just items you will use frequently for meals and recipes.

STEP **4**

Stick to the list. Once at the store, it's easy to go "off list" and end up spending money on items you don't need.

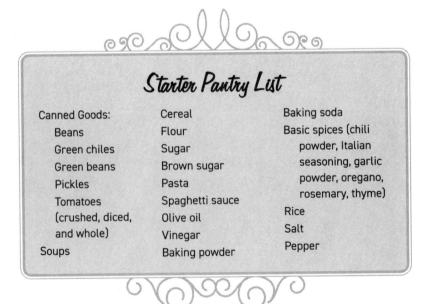

Starter Pantry List

Canned Goods:
- Beans
- Green chiles
- Green beans
- Pickles
- Tomatoes (crushed, diced, and whole)
- Soups

Cereal
Flour
Sugar
Brown sugar
Pasta
Spaghetti sauce
Olive oil
Vinegar
Baking powder

Baking soda
Basic spices (chili powder, Italian seasoning, garlic powder, oregano, rosemary, thyme)
Rice
Salt
Pepper

Brew Coffee

YOU WILL NEED:		TIME REQUIRED:
· Coffee brewer	· Coffee grinder (for beans)	15 minutes
· Whole bean or ground coffee	· Coffee filter	
	· Mug	

*L*ove the roasted bean? Going to a coffee shop for your caffeine fix can cost upwards of $4.00 a visit. That might be in your budget, but brew on this for a minute: making coffee at home can save you time, money, and the disappointment of walking out of a coffee shop only to find your drink less than awesome.

STEP **1**

Prep the brewer. Make sure the coffee brewer is clean and ready to brew.

STEP 2

Measure the water. Add cold water in the brewer's water reservoir to match the number of cups of coffee you want to drink.

STEP 3

Grind the beans. (Pre-ground coffee? Skip to STEP 4.) Fresh-ground coffee tastes best. Grind only the amount of beans you need for one brewing.

STEP 4

Replace the filter. Put a new coffee filter in the brewer.

STEP 5

Scoop the coffee. Measure and scoop coffee grounds into the coffee filter. Want a light-tasting brew? Use 1–1½ tablespoons ground coffee per 6 ounces of water. Bolder taste desired? Use 2–2½ tablespoons ground coffee per 6 ounces of water.

STEP 6

Start brewing. With the empty coffeepot under the filter, start the brewer.

STEP 7

Pour and embellish. Once the brewing process is complete, pour the coffee into your favorite mug and feel free to add sugar, flavored syrup, milk, cream, or even whipped cream to make this masterpiece your own!

STEP 8

Enjoy. Enjoy a cup of hot caffeinated (or decaffeinated) goodness.

Helpful Hint

Store coffee beans at room temperature in an airtight, opaque container. To ensure a fresh cup of brew, use any bag of beans within one week of opening.

Make Pancakes from Scratch

YOU WILL NEED:

- Ingredients
- Measuring cup
- Measuring spoons
- Large mixing bowl
- Mixing spoon
- Pan or griddle
- Flat spatula
- Stove top

TIME REQUIRED:

15 minutes

*W*arm and good for any time of the day, pancakes are easy to make and taste SO GOOD! It takes only a few minutes to mix up your own batter—you don't need a box. Find all the ingredients you need and show off your pancake-making skills . . . although your pancake-flipping talents may take some extra practice.

STEP **1**

Gather ingredients. This recipe makes eighteen 6″ pancakes or six "Supercakes."

3 cups all-purpose flour	3 cups buttermilk
3 tablespoons white sugar	½ cup milk
3 teaspoons baking powder	3 eggs
1½ teaspoons baking soda	⅓ cup melted butter
¾ teaspoon salt	

STEP 2

Mix dry ingredients. In a mixing bowl, stir together flour, sugar, baking powder, baking soda, and salt.

STEP 3

Mix in wet ingredients. Add the buttermilk, milk, eggs, and melted butter to the dry ingredients.

STEP 4

Stir ingredients. Evenly mix together the wet and dry ingredients until the batter is a smooth consistency and free from clumps.

STEP 5

Let the batter sit. Allow the batter to sit for five minutes before pouring. Seriously, this makes a difference.

STEP 6

Preheat the pan/griddle. On a stove-top burner set to medium heat, get your cook surface ready. When you sprinkle drops of water on the skillet and they sizzle, it's ready.

STEP 7

Cook pancakes. Prep the pan with a light coat of butter or cooking oil/ spray. Pour a desired amount of batter onto your pan or griddle. When bubbles form and pop on the upside of the cake, flip with the flat spatula to brown the other side.

Wise Woman

"Cheap pancakes taste cheap. Using buttermilk in your mix and letting the batter sit for five minutes before pouring makes a big difference in how your pancakes look and taste."

—Erica Catherman

Scramble Eggs

YOU WILL NEED:

- Fresh eggs
- Milk or water (just a splash, a teaspoon or so)
- Butter or cooking oil/spray
- Frying pan/skillet
- Mixing bowl
- Whisk or fork
- Spatula
- Stove top

TIME REQUIRED:

5 minutes

*E*ggs, in moderation, are a great source of protein and a good way to start your day. Add a piece of toast and/or half an avocado and it's even better! Scrambled eggs are the fastest egg prep option, almost as quick as a bowl of cereal.

STEP **1**

Break eggs. Crack open eggs into a mixing bowl. Try two eggs per person for a start. Add a teaspoon, or a splash, of milk or water to the eggs.

Scramble eggs. Use a whisk or fork to scramble the egg yolk and white together until they are one solid silky yellow color.

Heat pan. Over medium-high heat, preheat the pan on a stove-top burner.

> "My favorite thing to cook is eggs . . . from poached to soufflés!"
>
> —STACEY COATES,
> Head Pastry Chef,
> graduate of The Culinary
> Institute of America

Cook eggs. Prep the pan with a light coat of butter or cooking oil/spray. Pour the whisked eggs into the preheated pan. Using the spatula, mix the eggs in the pan until they solidify. After a few times, you will figure out what is underdone or overdone and how you like them best.

Enjoy breakfast. Transfer the cooked eggs to a plate, add salt and pepper to taste, and eat.

Did You Know?

Eggs have been served for breakfast for thousands of years. East India historians believe chickens were raised to lay eggs from as far back as 3200 BC. Seriously, they weren't yolking around.

Cook Bacon

YOU WILL NEED:	TIME REQUIRED:
· Raw bacon	10 minutes
· Frying pan	
· Cooking tongs	
· Paper towels	
· Stove top	

There are many ways to cook bacon. In the oven on a cookie sheet, on the grill, in a frying pan. Take your pick of cooking methods, because it's probably going to taste good however you cook it! Watch out for splattering or spilling hot bacon grease, especially in a frying pan.

<hr />

STEP **1**

Preheat pan. Over medium-high heat, preheat the frying pan. Do not cook bacon on high heat. The bacon will burn and so might your kitchen via a grease fire.

Add bacon strips. Lay each individual bacon strip side by side in the pan.

Wash hands. Always wash your hands after working with raw cuts of meat.

Flip bacon. Using cooking tongs, flip each bacon strip to cook evenly on each side.

> "I unfortunately still crave chicken McNuggets and bacon, which is the meat candy of the world."[4]
>
> —KATY PERRY, American singer and songwriter

Cook to taste. Some like their bacon chewy while some like it crispy. It's your bacon, so it's your choice.

Drip dry. Transfer cooked bacon onto several layers of paper towels. This allows the excess fat drippings to be absorbed by the paper towels.

Enjoy bacon. Once the strips are cooked to your liking, enjoy. Mmm . . . bacon.

More Info

Never pour bacon fat down the sink drain. It will congeal and potentially clog the pipe. Instead, let the drippings cool in the pan and transfer them into a container that can be put in the trash.

Boil Pasta

YOU WILL NEED:		TIME REQUIRED:
· Large pot	· Measuring spoon	15 minutes
· Colander	· Large spoon	
· Pasta	· Stove top	
· Salt		

*P*asta should be one of the easier meals to make, especially if you are not making homemade pasta dough. Once cooked to al dente, there are so many ways to use the pasta. Add marinara, meatballs, oil and vinegar, veggies, or even shrimp and eggs for a seafood carbonara. Getting hungry? Let's start with the pasta!

STEP 1

Boil water. Fill pot about ¾ full with water and bring to a boil on a stove-top burner. (Add a lid to bring it to a boil faster.)

Add salt. Measure and pour 1 teaspoon of salt into boiling water.

STEP 3

Measure serving size. Most types of pasta double in size once cooked. So, 1 cup uncooked pasta results in 2 cups cooked. A fistful of spaghetti results in dinner for two.

STEP 4

Add pasta. Slowly add pasta to boiling water, no lid needed. Most pasta will cook in 8–12 minutes. Read the package for the recommended cooking time.

STEP 5

Stir. Pasta will stick together if not stirred during the first few minutes of cooking.

STEP 6

Watch the heat. If the water in the pot begins to boil over, turn the burner heat down.

STEP 7

Test the pasta. Using a fork, fish a piece from the pot. Once cooled, bite through it. Properly cooked pasta is firm yet tender. This is called *al dente*. The color should be opaque cream all the way through.

STEP 8

Strain. Place a colander in the sink and pour in the pot of pasta. Remember the water and steam is hot, so don't get burned. Shake the colander to free any excess water from the pasta. And don't rinse the pasta; the starch that coats it gives it more flavor and helps sauce adhere to it.

More Info

A colander is a bowl-shaped kitchen utensil with holes in it, used for draining water from food, including pasta.

Cook Rice

YOU WILL NEED:

- Medium cooking pot with tight-fitting lid
- Rice
- Measuring cup
- Water
- Fork
- Stove top

TIME REQUIRED:

20–45 minutes (always read the directions on the package; different types of rice have different cooking times)

ice is easy to make and goes well with many different types of food. Be careful to follow directions so your rice doesn't end up too gummy or crunchy. Once you perfect the basics of cooking rice you can start adding your own twist to include additional ingredients like lime and cilantro or coconut milk and curry. So many options!

Boil water. Check the directions on the rice to determine the correct water-to-rice ratio for the number of servings you would like. Put the measured water into the pot, and if the package directions request it, add the rice now. Turn the stove-top burner on high and bring the water to a boil.

STEP **2**

Add rice. If you are supposed to add the rice *after* the water boils, do so now.

STEP **3**

Put the lid on. Once the water and rice have come to a boil, place a tight-fitting lid on the pot.

STEP **4**

Turn down the burner. As soon as you put the lid on the pot of rice and water, turn the burner down to simmer or low.

STEP **5**

Set timer. Set a timer for the amount of time required according to the directions on the rice package.

STEP **6**

Uncover and fluff the rice. When your timer goes off, turn off the burner and let the rice sit with the lid on for 5–10 minutes (again, there may be a recommended time on the rice package). Take the lid off the pan and use a fork to "fluff" the rice. Remember, the texture you're looking for is light and fluffy, not gummy or hard.

Fun Facts

June 29 is National Rice Day.
September is National Rice Month.
2004 was the International Year of Rice.

Make Mashed Potatoes

YOU WILL NEED:

- Potatoes (russet, 5–7 medium-sized)
- Cooking pot
- Colander
- Vegetable peeler
- Knife
- Potato masher or mixer
- Measuring cup
- Butter (2–6 tablespoons)
- Milk (½–¾ cup)
- Salt and pepper to taste
- Stove top

TIME REQUIRED:

35–45 minutes

ashed potatoes are a staple food on the tables of many Europeans, particularly in Ireland and Poland. But did you know potatoes are native to North America? They are. The starchy tuber was not introduced to Europe till 1526. Packed with carbs, the root can be grown year-round in many climates worldwide. Boiled, baked, fried, or smashed, the potato is the side dish of choice by people around the world.

STEP **1**

Prepare potatoes. Wash and peel the potatoes with the vegetable peeler, digging out the eyes with the end of the peeler.

Cut potatoes. Use a sharp knife to cut each potato into four to six even pieces and put them into a pot. Fill the pot with enough water to fully cover the potatoes.

STEP **3**

Cook the potatoes. On a stove-top burner, bring the water to a boil and then reduce the heat to a simmer. Simmer the potatoes for 15–20 minutes.

STEP **4**

Drain the potatoes. When the potatoes are tender enough to be easily pierced with a fork, remove them from the heat and drain them with the colander.

STEP **5**

Add other ingredients. Return your potatoes to the original pot. Add milk, butter, salt, and pepper to your preferred taste.

STEP **6**

Start mashing. Use a potato masher or mixer to mash the potatoes until they are creamy and free of lumps. Careful not to over-smash or over-mash, as the spuds will turn to a pasty glue if you do!

STEP **7**

Serve and enjoy.

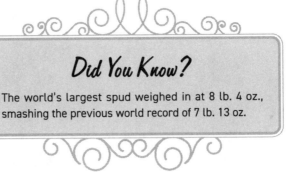

Did You Know?

The world's largest spud weighed in at 8 lb. 4 oz., smashing the previous world record of 7 lb. 13 oz.

Oven-Bake a Whole Chicken

YOU WILL NEED:

- Whole chicken
- Baking dish or roasting pan
- Olive oil or melted butter
- Salt and pepper, to taste
- Basting brush
- Aluminum foil
- Paper towels
- Meat thermometer
- Oven

TIME REQUIRED:

approximately 1 hour and 30 minutes

*C*ooked right, an oven-baked bird is a great meal to serve to friends, family, or anyone you want to invite over for a home-cooked meal. This method should give the bird a crispy skin without the added fat of frying and is delicious!

STEP **1**

Prepare the chicken. Ensure that the chicken is completely thawed. Remove and discard any giblets from the inner cavity. Pat the chicken dry with a paper towel. Put your chicken in a baking dish or roasting

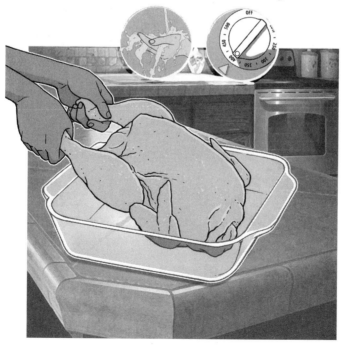

pan. Brush the chicken with melted butter or oil and season with salt and pepper. Cover the chicken with aluminum foil. Wash your hands to prevent the spread of germs.

STEP 2

Preheat oven to 400°F.

STEP 3

Cook the bird. Put the chicken in the center of the oven and cook for approximately 1 hour. If your chicken is larger than 3.5 pounds, add 10 minutes of cook time per pound. When the chicken has approximately 20 minutes of cook time remaining, remove the aluminum foil to allow the skin of the chicken to brown. Insert a meat thermometer into the thickest part of the chicken thigh. The chicken has finished cooking when the temperature reaches 165° and the juices from the chicken run clear.

STEP 4

Let rest. Once the chicken has reached the appropriate temperature, remove it from the oven and allow it to rest for 10 minutes. This allows the juices to redistribute throughout the chicken.

STEP 5

Clean up. While your chicken is resting, clean the kitchen and wash your hands.

STEP 6

Carve and serve. After your chicken has rested, carve the chicken and serve. Refrigerate any leftovers immediately.

Fact or Fiction:

There are more chickens than people on earth.

Fact. There are over 25 billion of them in the world—more than any other bird.

Broil Steak

YOU WILL NEED:

- Steak
- Oven
- Broiler pan
- Olive oil
- Steak seasonings
- Meat thermomete
- Oven

TIME REQUIRED:

Cook time 5–15 minutes

*B*roiled to perfection! No grill, no worries. Just follow these simple steps and you can quickly have your steak just the way you want it.

STEP **1**

Prepare your steak. Ensure that your steak is not frozen. Season both sides of your steak and allow it to rest at room temperature for 15 minutes.

Keep it clean. To avoid cross-contamination, never place cooked meat (or poultry or seafood) on a surface that had raw meat on it. And always wash your hands after handling raw meat, especially before handling other food. Same goes for utensils.

Prepare your oven. For electric ovens, adjust the top oven rack so that it is approximately 6 inches from the heating unit. For gas ovens, the broiler is sometimes located inside a separate pull-down door, usually above or below the oven. Turn your oven to "Broil" and put your broiler pan in to preheat it.

Broil your steak. Remove the hot broiler pan from your oven and position your steak in the center of the pan. For a cut of steak 1–1½″ thick, broil for 3–4 minutes on each side for rare, 5–6 minutes each side for medium, and 7–8 minutes each side for well done. The thickness of the steak may change the cooking times, so check the temperature of the meat to make sure it is done (directions under "Tips for Cooking Meat").

Let rest and enjoy. Remove your steak from the oven and allow it to rest for 5 to 8 minutes prior to cutting it. This allows the juices to redistribute into the steak. Your steak is now ready to enjoy.

Did You Know?

Your broiler may or may not have temperature settings: If ON or OFF are your only options, you can lower the cooking intensity by lowering the oven rack.

Tips for Cooking Meat

How would you like that cooked? When preparing beef or lamb you have choices about how long the meat is over/under the heat. Some people like their cut blood-rare while others prefer their meal to be mistaken for a charred black hockey puck. Near raw to near petrified, the choices vary as much as people's tastes.

Blue Rare—Barely cooked on the outside, center is cold and very red
Rare—Cooked on the very outside, center is cold and red
Medium Rare—Center is warm and red
Medium—Center is pink and firm
Medium Well—Center has very little pink
Well Done—Center is gray-brown

Is it done yet? The internal temperature, measured in Fahrenheit, determines the level of cooked or "done" a cut of meat is when fully prepared. The lower the internal temperature, the more rare the meat. The higher the internal temperature, the more thoroughly cooked the meat is when served. Keep in mind that most cuts of meat will still rise by 3°–5° after being removed from the heat source. Always serve pork and poultry at or above their "done" temperatures. Getting sick from undercooked meat is painful and the quickest way to convert to vegetarianism.

Beef	Lamb	Poultry
Blue Rare (less than 120°)	Rare (135°-140°)	Chicken (165°-175°)
Rare (120°-125°)	Medium Rare (140°-150°)	Turkey (165°-175°)
Medium Rare (125°-135°)	Medium (160°-165°)	**Pork**
Medium (135°-145°)	Medium Well (165° and above)	(145° or more)
Medium Well (145°-155°)		
Well Done (155° and more)		

Pan-Sear Fish

YOU WILL NEED:		TIME REQUIRED:
• Fish	• Frying pan	15–20 minutes
• Herbs or season-	• Olive oil	
ings, if desired	• Fork	
• Stove top	• Meat thermometer	

It's time to sear some salmon, or cod, or tilapia or whatever finned fish you wish. Cooked right, fish in the pan tastes great. Packed with omega-3 and vitamins such as D and B$_2$, fish is an easy way to bring a heart-healthy lite-meat balance to your dinner plate. Add a side of rice, fresh veggies, and some fresh fruit and you'll enjoy a healthy meal that can be plated in about 20 minutes.

STEP **1**

Prepare the fish. If you are using freshly filleted fish, check for and remove any remaining bones. If you are using a previously prepared filet, make sure your fish is not frozen.

Prepare the pan. Place the pan on the stove top and set the burner to medium-high. As the pan heats, spread a teaspoon of olive oil in the pan to prevent the fish from sticking.

Season as desired. Sprinkle fresh herbs or desired seasoning on the meat side of the fish.

Cook until done. Place the fish skin side down in the pan. After about 8 minutes, use a fork to poke down through to the thickest part of the fish to see if it has cooked all the way through. If it flakes apart and is opaque inside, it is done. The cooked temperature for fish is 145°F.

Remove and serve. Remove from the pan. Serve immediately.

More Info

Cooking fish with the skin on adds flavor and protects the meat from burning. You can remove the skin after cooking to make serving and eating easier.

Light a Charcoal Grill

YOU WILL NEED:

- Clean BBQ grill
- Charcoal briquettes
- Lighter fluid
- Matches or long-necked lighter

- Grill tools: spatula, tongs, basting brush, steak fork, a cleaning brush for the grill grate (for cleanup)

TIME REQUIRED:

5 minutes

Grilling is a fun way to cook food. It's great to grill for one or perfect for a party of people. You don't need the most expensive option, just a clean and functional grill. After each cookout make sure to give your grill a quick cleaning so it's ready the next time you want to "WOW" your guests with a wonderful meal.

STEP 1

Open vents. Open the grill's lower vents.

STEP 2

Remove top grate. Remove the cooking grill.

> "I love grilling anything on charcoal; vegetables, meat, fish. It creates the best flavor."
>
> —BRITTEN SHELSON, graduate of The Culinary Institute of America

STEP 3

Stack the charcoal. Create a pyramid shape on the bottom grate by stacking the briquettes 6″ high by 10″ across.

STEP 4

Douse the pyramid with lighter fluid. Use an evenly spread douse of about ½ cup of lighter fluid (read manufacturer's specification on the back of the charcoal bag).

STEP 5

Let lighter fluid absorb. Do not ignite the briquettes for 1 full minute after STEP 4. This ensures an even flame and avoids the dangers of an explosive flash ignition.

Ignite the pyramid of briquettes. Stand with your face and body turned away from the grill, and ignite the briquettes from the base of the stack. Small flames will move up the pyramid while smoke begins to appear from within.

Let the briquettes burn undisturbed. Within 10–15 minutes the briquettes will be covered with a white/gray ash while the center of the stack glows red-hot.

Spread the hot briquettes. Use a long-handled metal tool to spread the hot briquettes evenly over the bottom grate.

Replace the cooking grill. Allow the cooking grill to heat up prior to placing your food over the heat.

Grill your food. Beef, chicken, pork, fish, veggies, and fruits like peaches and apples taste great grilled. It's your choice.

Clean it up. Once your grill has cooled and your guests are gone, use that cool cleaning brush to scrape down the grill grate. Get off all the cooked-on food bits before closing the grill lid.

More Info

WARNING! NEVER EVER spray lighter fluid on a lit fire. The flame could travel up the spray-stream and ignite the bottle, causing a serious or life-threatening burn injury.

Grill Steak

YOU WILL NEED:		TIME REQUIRED:
· Selected cut of steak	· Meat thermometer	6–20 minutes (after
· Preheated grill	· Olive oil	steaks sit at room
· Long-handled BBQ	· Steak seasonings	temperature)
utensils, tongs, or fork		

*T*here has long been debate about what cooking method is best for steak. Whatever your preference, the grill is a great way to go. The char from the fire, cooking outside, the grill marks on the steak . . . okay, I'm hungry! Let's grill a steak!

STEP **1**

Prepare your steak. Ensure that your steak is not frozen. Allow the meat to rest at room temperature for 15 minutes before grilling.

Season to taste. Brush both sides of the steak with olive oil and season with selected spices. An even mix of salt and pepper is a good start.

STEP **3**

Sear the outside. Use BBQ utensils to place the steak over the hottest spot on the grill. When grilling a steak 1–1½″ thick, sear one side at a time for 2–4 minutes per side, until the outside is golden brown to lightly charred (or seared). Your seared steak is now officially rare.

STEP **4**

Cook the inside. Move the steak to a cooler space on the grill and cook 3–5 minutes per side for medium rare (internal temp of 135°F), 5–7 minutes = medium (internal temp of 140°F), 7–10 minutes = medium well (150°F).

STEP **5**

Enjoy. Straight from the grill or after letting the cut rest for a few minutes, your steak is ready to eat.

Wise Woman

"The only time to eat diet food is while you're waiting for the steak to cook."[5]

—Julia Child, American chef, author, and television personality

Know Your Cuts of Steak

Not all steaks are created equal. Before you head to the butcher's, know what you plan on sinking your teeth into. Learning the names and cuts of meat can be the difference between enjoying a steak that melts in your mouth and suffering through one that chews like leather.

Tenderloin—Also known as a filet or filet mignon, this cut is often considered the "special occasion" steak. Because the area of the cow it comes from doesn't do much work, it remains extremely tender. Cook properly and you will be able to cut this steak with a fork.

Cost—$$$$
Tenderness—Very
Marble—Low
Flavor—Medium

Strip Steak—Also called a New York strip or a Kansas City cut, this meat is perfect for grilling on any occasion. A half-inch of fat usually runs along one side of the steak. Trim this off after grilling so the full flavor of the marbling cooks into the meat.

Cost—$$$
Tenderness—Very
Marble—High
Flavor—Full

Rib Eye—Cut from the center portion of the cow's rib section, the rib eye is a very favorable steak. Cook properly and each juicy bite will seem to melt in your mouth.

Cost—$$$
Tenderness—Very
Marble—High
Flavor—Medium

T-Bone/Porterhouse—This is really two steaks in one. On either side of the T-shaped bone are different types of meat: a strip steak on one side and tenderloin on the other. Keep in mind that the bone affects the way the meat cooks. The portion closer to the bone cooks slower. This means the cut can cook rare to medium at the bone and well to well done on the edges.

Cost—$$$
Tenderness—Very
Marble—Low on the tenderloin
    side, High on the strip side
Flavor—Medium to Full

Sirloin—Not the best grill steak. This is because sirloin is cut from high on the cow's rear, back where the muscle is well used. It's good as stew meat or sliced into cubes and cooked with vegetables on a kabob.

Cost —$$
Tenderness—Low
Marble—Lean
Flavor—Medium

Tri Tip—Seasoned or marinated first, this cut is best cooked at low temperatures over an extended period of time. It is most often served sliced an eighth- to quarter-inch thick and cut across the grain of the meat.

Cost—$$
Tenderness—Low
Marble—Lean
Flavor—Full

Flank—Flank steak comes from a very strong, well-exercised part of the cow's lower abdominal muscle. This makes it a tough meat that is best sliced across the grain when serving. Dry rub seasoning or marinating the meat overnight will help tenderize the cut.

Cost—$
Tenderness—Low
Marble—Lean
Flavor—Medium

Skirt—This cut comes from the plate of the cow. Located below the ribs and in front of the flank, the skirt steak is long, flat, and enjoyed for its flavor, not tenderness. It is best sliced across the grain when serving.

Cost—$
Tenderness—Low
Marble—Lean
Flavor—Full

Grill Pork Chops

YOU WILL NEED:		TIME REQUIRED:
· Grill	· Aluminum foil	20-30 minutes
· Pork chops	· Plate	
(boneless)	· Meat	
· Tongs	thermometer	

*P*ork. Known as "the other white meat," pork is one of the most commonly consumed meats in the world. History holds records of pig farmers dating back to 5000 BC. Tender and flavorful pork chops are good eats any time of the year. Just be mindful of how much you pig out. Savor the swine too much and you'll move to the front of the line for heart disease. Yet pig heart valves have been used to replace damaged human heart valves, so maybe the same pig that ruins a heart can also fix it.

Fire up the grill. Heat your grill to medium/hot, which is 350°–375°. While your grill is preheating, allow the pork chops to rest at room temperature to ensure even cooking.

Place the chops on the grill. Using tongs, place the pork chops on the grill and close the lid.

Rotate them 45°. After 2 minutes turn the pork chops 45°. Close the lid for 2 more minutes.

Flip them over. Use your tongs to flip over the pork chops. Repeat STEP 3. Total cook time for ¾″ chops is 8–12 minutes. Use a meat thermometer to check that the internal temperature is at least 145°.

Let 'em rest. Remove the pork chops from the grill and place them on a plate. Cover them with aluminum foil for 5 minutes before serving.

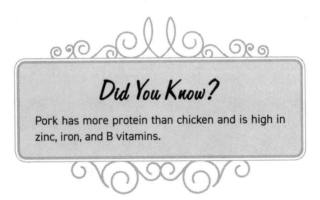

Did You Know?

Pork has more protein than chicken and is high in zinc, iron, and B vitamins.

Sharpen a Kitchen Knife

YOU WILL NEED:
- Knife
- Sharpening stone
- Mineral oil

TIME REQUIRED:
1–5 minutes

*M*uch can be saved when a knife is kept sharp. A sharp edge saves time, energy, and frustration. It also saves you from experiencing the agony of dull steel not cutting through tough bread yet slicing into your soft finger with ease. Save yourself the pain by carving out a few minutes once a month to carefully sharpen the kitchen knives. Your food will not only look better cleanly sliced and diced, it will taste better knowing no fingers were sacrificed in the meal prep.

STEP 1

Prepare the stone. On the rough side of the sharpening stone, add an ample amount of mineral oil across the entire surface of the stone.

Angle the blade. Hold the knife to the face of the stone at an angle between 10° and 20°.

Sharpen the first side. Touch the blade flat on the sharpening stone at the desired angle. Keeping the angle steady, drag the knife across the stone while applying moderate pressure. Repeat this 8–10 times per side.

Sharpen the second side. Flip the blade to the other side and repeat the sharpening process.

Repeat with fine stone. Flip over the sharpening stone and repeat the process using the fine finish side of the stone. This ensures a smooth cutting edge across the entire surface of the blade.

Test the blade. Cut into a piece of fruit or firm vegetable to test the blade. If you are satisfied with the cutting edge, congratulations. If a sharper blade is desired, return to STEP 3.

Wise Woman

"A sharp knife is a chef's best friend."

—Ancient proverb

10

Tools & Fix-It

*I've given up on the idea,
on any preconception,
that there is a limit to
what is appropriate or
accessible to girls.*

—EMILY PILLOTON,
designer, author, speaker, entrepreneur

*T*oday's sawdust swept from the concrete floor is evidence of work well done. Tomorrow's MIG (metal inert gas) welding sparks will again prove there's nothing a girl can't build. With the motto "Fear Less. Build More." Girls Garage is much greater than a physical place where girls ages 9–17 spend time with friends after school or in summer programs. The 3,600-square-foot fully functional workspace in Berkeley, California, draws in girl designers and builders seeking the know-how to fuse metal, make trouble, speak up, and stand out!

Emily Pilloton is the founder and executive director of the nonprofit Project H Design and Girls Garage. Never one to shy away from getting dirt under her fingernails, Emily has a girls-can-do-anything attitude that has earned her the TED Talk stage, a guest seat on the Colbert Report, print in the *New York Times*, published books, and much more. Years in the making, Emily's interest in design and building dates back as far as she can remember. "I've always been drawn to the act of making and the mechanical side of life. From when I was little I liked taking things apart, looking at gears, and figuring out how things work in the physical world."[1]

Thinking back to high school, Emily proudly describes her teen-self as "a huge math nerd." At the same time, she genuinely enjoyed her other classes. When she discovered architecture, Emily found herself geeking out by the intersection of all her school subjects. It was like everything she was learning merged together. "You had to know how to do math and why things stood up or fell down. You had to know the social context of where you are building and how to talk to other humans."

Emily was drawn into architecture as a way of joining the technical side of building and the creative side of design. This led the young creator to her first big builds when, as an 11th grader, she founded one of the first Habitat for Humanity high school campus chapters. This gave her tool time on real projects, which only hammered home her personal drive to do more. Next, Emily fund-raised enough to spend the summer in Belize working on building projects. Through pouring concrete, cutting rebar, and serving the needs of others, Emily reached her tipping point. She told herself, "Okay, I got it. This is what I want to do." So, she spent years creating a value system around what that could mean in her life. "I carefully considered the intersection of design and building and why working with humans and not just detailing plumbing fixtures on AutoCAD was important to me. This really helped me make sense of the work, how my brain thinks, and how I could put my energy into what feels productive."

Looking back, Emily had multiple mentors who showed her how being creative and having dirty hands went well together. From a high school environmental science teacher who held project-based classes outside in the wetlands, to the hardcore focus and dedication of both her grandmothers, Emily learned the value of being a hardworking, independent woman who's also engaged in creative practices. "I've given up on the idea, on any preconception, that there is a limit to what is appropriate or accessible to girls." Emily deconstructs barriers that hold girls back by assembling teams of talented and tenacious women who are experts in their fields and are willing to share their skills and character with young girls. Each woman designer and builder exemplifies the love, grit, and all-around know-how they nurture in the girls they teach. This makes Girls Garage a safe space to be creative, experiment, and inspire learning in the next generation of women in the making. From this blueprint, Emily shares with all those who call Girls Garage their garage: "Learning is incremental and there is always the next thing to learn."

Looking forward, Emily wonders, will the girls she's teaching to cut and weld, wrench and hammer be the next generation of designers and builders? Will those girls with dirty hands and creative minds see Emily and the women of Girls Garage as the kind of mentors that built into them the skills and character of confident, capable women? How can they not?

Stock a Tool Kit

YOU WILL NEED:
· See tools listed below

TIME REQUIRED:
30 minutes to a lifetime

*B*uilding a collection of tools will come in handy when you want to hang a picture or need to turn off a leaking water valve. Using the right tool for the job is the best way to complete build-it/fix-it tasks when quality matters. Using the wrong tool for the task is the fastest way to frustration, damage, and added expense to the project. Your best bet is to stock your first tool kit with the basics and build up from there. Here's how to get started.

STEP 1

Select the tools. A poor craftsman blames their tools, yet cheap tools are seldom worth keeping. Buy your tools from a quality supply store, or accept a donation from someone who knows their tools.

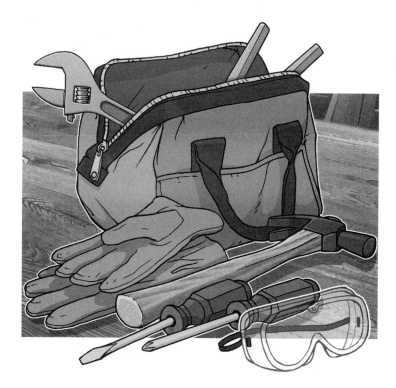

Organize the tools. Keep your tools organized in your tool box/bag so you'll always know where to find them when you need them.

Use the tools. Hammers are intended to pound nails and wrenches are not. Use your tools properly and they'll serve you well for years to come.

Build your tool selection. It's a good idea to build your tool kit up over time. When you need a specific tool, purchase it and keep it handy.

Here are fifty tools any Do-It-Yourselfer can take pride in owning:

1. Adjustable wrench (aka Crescent wrench)
2. Brooms (both standard angle and large push)
3. C-clamps
4. Caulk gun
5. Chalk reel
6. Chisels
7. Chop saw
8. Circular saw
9. Combination square
10. Cordless drill
11. Crowbar
12. Drill (corded)
13. Drill bits (for metal & wood)
14. Duct tape
15. Dust mask
16. Dust broom (small hand-held)
17. Dustpan
18. Earplugs
19. Electrical tape
20. Extension cord
21. Flashlight
22. Hammer
23. Hand saws (wood & metal)
24. Hex/Allen key set
25. Jigsaw
26. Ladder
27. Level
28. Open-end/box-end wrenches (standard & metric)
29. Pipe wrench
30. Pliers (Channellock & needle-nose)
31. Plungers (sink & toilet)
32. Reciprocal saw
33. Safety glasses
34. Sandpaper
35. Sanding block
36. Screwdrivers (flathead & Phillips)
37. Socket set (standard & metric)
38. Step stool
39. Stud finder

40. Table saw
41. Tape measure
42. Utility knife
43. Utility snips
44. Vise-grips
45. Voltmeter

46. Wire cutters
47. Wire strippers
48. Wood glue
49. Work light
50. 1½″ putty knife

Did You Know?

A weaver in Harvard Massachusetts named Tabitha Babbitt was the first to suggest that lumber workers use a circular saw instead of the two-man pit saw. She made a prototype and attached it to her spinning wheel in 1813. Her invention is know worldwide as the circular saw.[2]

Read a Tape Measure

YOU WILL NEED:
· Retractable tape measure

TIME REQUIRED:
1 minute of practice now, 5 seconds later

*M*easure twice, cut once. And when the material is expensive, measure three times. Measuring something is a seemingly easy task, but if you ever cut something too short, you will realize being careful while you measure is important. Even when shopping for furniture. You need to know if that desk you love will actually fit in your room in the space you have available. Check your work before you cut something or make a furniture purchase!

STEP **1**

Extend tape measure. Pull the end hook to extend the tape measure several feet.

STEP **2**

Lock tape measure. Press the automatic rewind switch into the locked position.

STEP **3**

Measuring feet. The tape's measurements count up in 1-foot increments from the end hook. Each foot measurement is clearly printed in bold and marked by a line through the tape face.

STEP **4**

Measuring inches. Within each foot are inch measurements marked by a solid line through the tape's face.

STEP **5**

Measuring ½ inch. Within each inch measurement is a half-inch line.

STEP **6**

Measuring ¼ inch. Within each half-inch measurement is a quarter-inch line.

STEP **7**

Measuring ⅛ inch. Within each quarter-inch measurement is an eighth-inch line.

STEP **8**

Measuring ¹⁄₁₆ inch. Within each eighth-inch measurement is a sixteenth-inch line.

STEP **9**

Retract tape measure. Release the automatic rewind switch.

More Info

Many tape measures have marks every 16 inches. These indicate the standard distance between wall studs in a home's framing.

Swing a Hammer

YOU WILL NEED:
- Hammer
- Nail
- Board

TIME REQUIRED:
3 seconds

*H*itting a nail on the head is good. Otherwise you are probably smashing a finger or damaging whatever you intend to drive the nail into. Before you try to hammer a nail into something you care about, pound a few into a board that can take a few dents. The practice should pay off and soon you'll be hitting the nail on the head every time!

STEP 1

Get a grip. With a firm grip, hold the hammer toward the end of the handle. Hold the handle tight enough that the hammer will not slip from your grip.

Take aim. Focus on the exact spot you want to strike with the hammer's face. Keep your eyes focused on the head of the nail as you swing the hammer.

Swing away. Lock your wrist and use the strength of your arm and elbow's extension to swing the hammer to directly strike the nail's head.

TIP:

If the nail bends, the face of the hammer is striking the nail's head at an angle. Pull the nail out and start again. The proper strike occurs when the nail's head and hammer's face meet flush, without any angle at the point of contact.

Drive it home. After hitting the nail once, raise the hammer and swing again until the nail is driven to the desired depth.

Did You Know?

There are two types of claw hammers. The curved claw hammer is designed for low impact, finessed nail pulling. The straight claw hammer is made to pry and tear nails free, demo style.

Cut with a Circular Saw

YOU WILL NEED:		TIME REQUIRED:
· Circular saw	· Straight edge	1–3 minutes (Depends on
· Lumber to cut	· Cutting surface	a few factors: What are
· Measuring tape	· Safety glasses	you cutting? Is the blade of
· Pencil	· Earplugs	your circular saw sharp?)

*L*ike to DIY? "Do It Yourself" projects can be fun and leave you with a feeling of accomplishment. A circular saw is a tool you'll need to master to help you build that desk you've always wanted or construct something even bigger, like that house you're dreaming about.

STEP **1**

Mark your cut line. Measure and mark the line you plan to cut. Use a straight edge and pencil to mark the line you will follow with the guide on the saw.

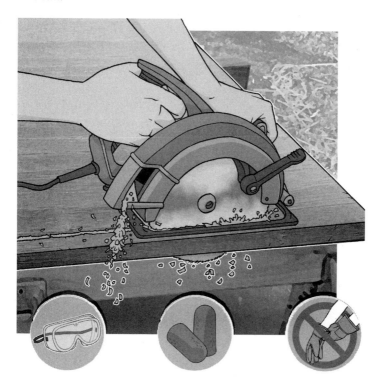

Prep the lumber. Place the lumber securely on a surface in a way that the end you are cutting off will fall free. This may require clamping down or having a partner safely hold down the lumber opposite from the end you are cutting off. Check to make sure the blade of the saw cutting through the bottom of the lumber will not come in contact with any other material.

Put safety first. Insert earplugs and put on your safety glasses. Do not wear gloves, as you need to maintain dexterity and avoid glove fabric getting pulled into the blade.

Prepare to cut. Rest the front of the saw (called the shoe) on the material you are about to cut. Make sure the blade is not touching the material. Position the cut guide marked on the shoe to the blade's cut path marked in pencil on the material.

Cut. Pull the trigger on the saw. When the saw blade has reached full speed, start to push the saw away from your body and into the material you are cutting. Follow the cut guide on the shoe and the edge of the blade along the cut path marked in pencil.

Complete the cut. Continue pushing the running saw through the material following the line you drew. As you approach the far side of the board and the end of your cut, make sure you are clear of the piece about to fall to the floor.

Stop the cut. Remove your finger from the trigger to stop the saw. Hold the saw in one place while the blade stops spinning. Once the saw has stopped completely, set it aside in a safe location.

Wise Woman

"If it's going to kill you, don't do it, leave that to a licensed professional. Or if it requires a license, you have to check with your city. Your electrical service, that will kill you. Don't do it. But something simple like changing a light fixture, you can do that. Easy stuff like that. That's the only way I learned, it was by trying everything."[3]

—Nicole Curtis, host of HGTV's *Rehab Addict*

Use a Drill

YOU WILL NEED:

· Drill   · Pencil
· Drill bit   · Safety glasses

TIME REQUIRED:

2–5 minutes

Cordless drills have come a long way since they first showed up on construction sites. Today's drill packs powerful torque into a small package of precision. You'll find them handy in a variety of scenarios—from small projects around the house to building a home. Whether hanging a coat hook or boring through brick, knowing how to work a drill is a must for the DIY and pro alike.

STEP 1

X marks the spot. Determine where you wish to drill a hole and mark an X in the exact spot with a pencil.

STEP 2

Check around. Look behind, under, and around the area you want to drill the hole. Ask yourself, "Is there anything behind or under the X that my drill bit can damage?" Look for pipes, nails, wiring, the countertop, your hand, or your friend's hand. And never wear loose clothing or jewelry that could get caught if you lean in too close.

STEP 3

Select a bit. Choose a drill bit appropriate to the material you are drilling through. Different bits are designed for different materials. Check the bit case for the material it is designed to drill through.

STEP 4

Secure the bit. Place the bit into the end of the drill and tighten the keyless chuck. Some older and many large industrial power drills require securing the bit in place with a chuck key.

Start the hole. Put on your safety glasses before drilling. Place the tip of the drill bit in contact with your material and slowly pull the trigger. Go slow and remember the material you are drilling through determines the proper drill speed. Forcing your way through hard material will dull the bit and even burn the material.

Reverse directions. Once you have successfully drilled through the material, stop the drill. If the bit is stuck in the material, flip the direction switch into reverse. Slowly pull the trigger and reverse the bit back out through the material.

Did You Know?

A drill can also be used as an electric screwdriver. With the proper bit attachment (purchase at any hardware store), you can quickly screw in or reverse out Phillips or flathead screws. Just go slow. With all that power, it is easy to over-torque and even strip your materials.

Use a Crowbar

YOU WILL NEED:
- Crowbar
- Items that need pulling, prying, or separating

TIME REQUIRED:
1–60 seconds

*W*recking bar, pry bar, pinch-bar, jimmy bar, gooseneck, or pig foot are some names used for the crowbar. Among the simplest, oldest, and toughest devices in history, the crowbar remains a great tool to own. More than a mindless muscle power tool, a crowbar requires some practiced skill and careful finesse to use properly. Leverage the steel correctly and you will pry your way through difficult jobs with ease.

STEP **1**

Wear gloves. No matter what you are doing with the crowbar, you will need to grasp the crowbar firmly.

Pull nails. Use the sharply curved end of the crowbar to pull nails. Hook the head of the nail with the notched end of the tool. Lever the nail out by rolling the tool along the sharp curve.

CAUTION:

As you pull nails, the material beneath the crowbar's sharp curve can dent or mark as pressure beneath the tool is greatest here. To avoid damage while prying, a scrap of wood can be placed between the crowbar and the surface you want to protect.

Pry apart. If you are separating two pieces of wood by prying them apart, use the long end with the flat tip. Insert the end of the crowbar as far between the two pieces as possible. Leverage the crowbar on the slight bend of the chisel tip to separate the two pieces. Continue to push the crowbar into the space you create and repeat the prying motion.

Did You Know?

A crowbar is used in the play *Romeo and Juliet* (Act 5, Scene 2, Lines 17–22).

FRIAR LAURENCE
    Unhappy fortune! by my brother,
    The letter was not nice but full of change
    Of dear important, and the neglecting it
    May do much danger. Friar John, go hence;
    Get me an iron crow, and bring it straight
    Unto my cell.

Use an Adjustable Wrench

YOU WILL NEED:
- Adjustable (Crescent) wrench
- A bolt or nut in need of turning

TIME REQUIRED:
30 seconds to 1 minute

*C*alled an adjustable spanner, adjustable Crescent, or adjustable wrench, this tool is used to tighten or loosen a nut or bolt that you might find on a bicycle, a toilet, a car, or any furniture that requires assembly. Often referred to as a Crescent wrench, due to the original manufacturer, the adjustable wrench is a staple of every useful toolbox and has been so for over a century. Proper use of an adjustable wrench can save a day, while improper use can end up with the head of a bolt rounded and your knuckles smashed.

STEP **1**

Open the jaws. Use your thumb and finger to twist open the thumbscrew. This will adjust the jaws of the wrench to the approximate size of the bolt/nut head.

Position the wrench. Slide the open jaws of the wrench around the bolt/nut. If the jaws aren't open enough to slide over the head, make another adjustment.

Tighten the jaws. Twist tight the jaws of the wrench until both sides are firmly seated against two sides of the bolt/nut. "Meatloaf knuckles" are caused by the wrench slipping off the bolt/nut and your hand smashing into an adjacent surface. Help prevent meatloaf knuckles by seating the wrench all the way down on the bolt/nut.

Rotate. Rotate the bolt/nut in the direction desired. As silly as it sounds, a good way to remember which way to turn the bolt/nut is "righty tighty, lefty loosey."

Did You Know?

Wrench is an American term for the tool. It is also known as a *spanner*, especially in British English, or a *spanner wrench*.

Use a Level

YOU WILL NEED:
· 3-bubble level

TIME REQUIRED:
15 seconds

*W*hen you need something to be exactly level (horizontal) or plumb (vertical), it's important to use a level. When hanging a picture, a level will keep heads from tilting to the side while looking at the frame—unless they are contemplating the artwork!

STEP **1**

Pick a bubble. Better levels have 3 bubble vials. One is for checking a horizontal grade. One is for checking a vertical grade. The third (not used as often) is set diagonally in the level and is used for finding a 45-degree angle.

Check for *level*. Place the tool horizontally (on its side). You want to observe the bubble vial that is also horizontal. If the bubble in the vial is exactly between the two lines, the item can be considered *level*. If the bubble is outside of the lines, adjust your object until the horizontal bubble rests between the lines.

Check for *plumb*. *Plumb* describes an item standing perfectly straight up and down (vertical). Hold the level against an item vertically and observe the vial sitting horizontally. If the bubble rests exactly between the two lines, the item is considered plumb. If the bubble is not between the two lines, adjust the item accordingly.

Check for *angle*. The diagonal vial on the level will tell you if an item is at a 45-degree angle. If the bubble is between the two lines when the level is resting on the item, it is close to 45 degrees. If not between the lines, adjust the item until the bubble rests between the lines.

Fun Fact

The bubble level is considered a relatively new tool. The ancient Egyptians built the Great Pyramids to exact specifications using a simple yet highly effective A-frame structure made of three pieces of wood and weighted string.

Calculate Square Footage

YOU WILL NEED:
- Tape measure
- Pencil and paper or calculator

TIME REQUIRED:
Depending on the size of the room(s), probably about 5 minutes

"When will I ever use this math?" you once asked yourself in the middle of math class. Well, today is when. As easy as simple algebra (L × W = SF), calculating square footage is simple. Get it right and all those math classes just paid off. Get it wrong and you may buy too much material or, even worse, too little. Getting it just right gives you the power to get your task done right whether building something or fitting square footage "A" into square footage "B."

STEP **1**

Measure the length. From one end of the room to the other, measure the room's length.

Measure the width. From one side of the room to the other, measure the room's width.

Multiply the two. Length × Width = Square Footage (L × W = SF).

More Info

If the room is not square, as they rarely are, picture the room as numerous squares and rectangles. For example: An L-shaped room could be broken into one long rectangle and a square. Figure the square footage of the rectangle and then the square footage of the square. Add them together for the total square footage of the room.

Turn Off a Toilet Water Line

YOU WILL NEED:
· Your hand

TIME REQUIRED:
5 seconds

*Y*ou just used the toilet. After flushing, not everything has gone down the drain. To make matters worse, the water level is rising dangerously close to the top of the bowl. Something bad has happened down in the toilet's pipe, and as you stand there bug-eyed, you realize the situation is about to get worse. Much worse, if you don't act fast.

STEP **1**

Find the line. Look underneath the tank of the toilet for a water line. The water line will run from the tank of the toilet to the wall.

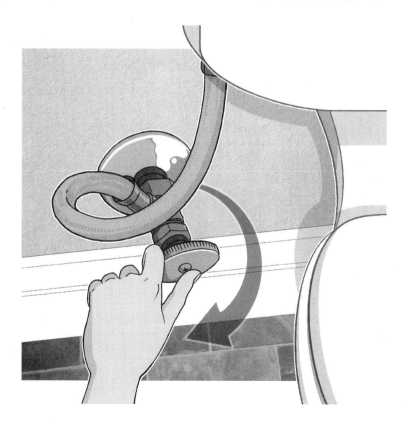

Locate the shutoff valve. At the end of the water line running from the toilet to the wall will be a shutoff valve sticking out of the wall. The water line will connect to this valve.

Turn the water line off. Standard shutoff valves work just like the valve attached to your garden hose. Turn the valve clockwise until it no longer turns. At this point the water in the bowl should stop rising. Catastrophe averted.

Read the instructions on "How to Unclog a Toilet."

Fact or Fiction:

Toilet paper overload is the #1 cause of toilet clogs.

Fact. Courtesy flushes while you are using the restroom can help to prevent a clog if you like using a lot of toilet paper. It should also be noted that not all insurance companies cover damage caused by toilet-paper-clogged drains. So that courtesy flush could also save thousands of dollars.

Unclog a Toilet

YOU WILL NEED:	TIME REQUIRED:
• Plunger (specifically a toilet plunger) • Plastic garbage bag • Paper towels	1–5 minutes

*I*f you use a toilet, at some point in life (if you can read this you are at that point) you should learn how to unclog a toilet. Toilet clogs happen from time to time. Usually due to too much of something or the wrong thing being flushed down the toilet. When you hit the jackpot of "the clogged pot," don't run away. Power up and unclog that pot!

STEP **1**

Turn off the water. If water in the bowl is getting close to the bowl's rim, turn off the water line behind the toilet. This will stop only the new

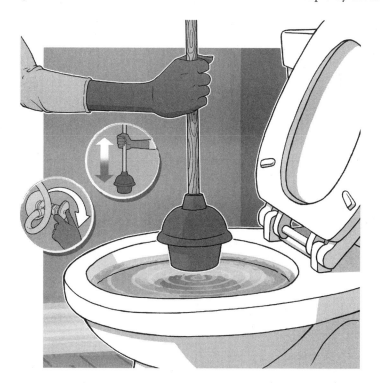

water from filling the tank and bowl. (See "How to Turn Off a Toilet Water Line.")

STEP 2

Use the proper plunger. Make sure the plunger you use is a toilet plunger as opposed to a sink plunger. (See "Helpful Hint" in "How to Clear a Clogged Sink Drain.")

STEP 3

Insert the plunger. Submerge the plunger into the toilet. If there is water standing in the bowl, this is good; water does not compress and will give you more applied force to the clog than if plunging with only air.

STEP 4

Plunge. Compress the plunger slowly at first. Plunging too vigorously could cause water to fly out of the bowl. For many reasons, you want the water to stay in the bowl.

STEP 5

Repeat plunging. Compress the plunger numerous times before removing the plunger head from the toilet. If the water in the toilet bowl drains freely, you have cleared the clog.

STEP 6

Turn on the water.

STEP 7

Clean up. After rinsing the plunger in the freshly flushed toilet bowl, put the plunger into the plastic bag. This will keep people from having a problem with you walking through the house with a wet toilet plunger.

STEP 8

Wash your hands. Always, always wash your hands after plunging a toilet.

Did You Know?

Long before flushing toilets, chamber pots were used to "relieve" oneself indoors. Once the chamber pot was used, the "contents" were tossed (often out the window).

Clear a Clogged Sink Drain

YOU WILL NEED:

- Plunger (specifically a sink plunger)
- Channellock pliers or pipe wrench
- Bucket to catch water from drain
- Rags/paper towels/old rag
- Cinnamon gum

TIME REQUIRED:

5–30 minutes

*T*his is most likely going to be gross. The degree of gross usually depends on where the sink is located. The kitchen sink will be gross, but clogged food particles are not too bad. Your bathroom sink is going to be grosser. Decomposing hair clogs and toothpaste slime tend to trigger the gag reflex. Regardless, with the following "how to," you have the power to free the drain of gross . . . or not so gross.

STEP 1

Plug the sink spill hole. Use an old rag to block the sink spill hole. This will keep plunged water from shooting out of the hole.

STEP 2

Plunge. Using a sink plunger, plunge clear the clog. If this fails to drain the sink, continue to STEP 3.

STEP 3

Locate the P-trap. Don't let the name fool you as the P-trap is the section of curved drainpipe shaped like a J. Think of it this way: the P-trap holds just enough water in the pipe to block sewer gases from coming back up through the sink's drain.

STEP 4

Chew gum. Insert a couple of pieces of cinnamon gum into your mouth. Remember the sewer gases mentioned in STEP 3? You're about to smell them, and cinnamon gum might keep you from gagging. Probably not, but it's worth a try.

STEP 5

Prep space. Put a bucket under the P-trap to catch the clogged water and nasty stuff that is about to spill out of the drainpipe.

STEP 6

Loosen nuts. The P-trap has two nuts, one on either side. Since this is designed to be installed by hand, you should be able to loosen these nuts and remove the trap easily. If they are too tight, use the Channellock pliers or pipe wrench.

CAUTION:
Any clogged water is about to spill violently out into the bucket.

STEP 7

Clear pipes. This step can get nasty, but you really must do it. Clean the drain and P-trap of any clogs. This may require the use of your finger or improvised use of a wire coat hanger.

Replace P-trap. When the drain and P-trap are clear, replace the P-trap and tighten the nuts.

Check for leaks. Run water through the drain and make certain the newly cleared pipes do not leak.

Helpful Hint

Sink plungers and toilet plungers are designed differently. A sink plunger looks like a ball cut in half with a stick on the end. It has a flat bottom designed to seal over a sink's drain. The toilet plunger includes an extra flange on the open end of the ball. This flange is designed to seal down into and force water through the toilet's drain.

Check the Circuit Breakers

YOU WILL NEED:
- Flashlight
- Dry hands
- Circuit breaker box

TIME REQUIRED:
1–3 minutes

*A*ll houses have a circuit box that controls the flow of electricity into and through the home. Usually located in a closet, utility room, or garage space, the circuit breaker box houses multiple individual circuit breakers. Each circuit breaker regulates the "juice" that flows through wires to outlets, switches, and appliances. When too much electricity is drawn down a wire (usually because too many electronic devices are plugged into one circuit), the circuit "flips" or shuts off automatically. This is a good thing, considering the alternative is a literal meltdown and potential fire. Most sane people don't want this to happen. When electricity flows exceed safe limits, the circuit flips off and will require you to manually reset the individual breaker. Don't worry—the process of resetting the flipped

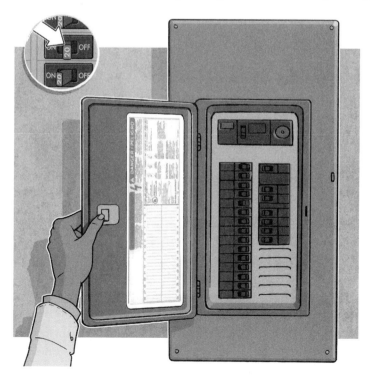

circuit and restoring power to your phone charger or hair dryer is simple and safe. Just don't do it with wet hands. Shocking!

STEP 1

Locate the circuit breaker box. Look in the garage, utility room, or closet for a flat metal panel with a metal door.

STEP 2

Open the door. Unlatch the door and open fully.

STEP 3

Examine the circuits. Look at the rows of switches. One will be flipped away from the ON position. Rather than flipping fully into the OFF position, it will be halfway between ON and OFF. This is the circuit that needs to be reset.

STEP 4

Flip to ON. Push the switch of the individually flipped circuit all the way OFF and then back to the ON position. (If the circuit will not stay on, there is probably a serious problem. You will need to contact a professional electrician.)

STEP 5

Close the door. Once the circuit has been reset, close the door and enjoy the juice.

Wise Woman

"Know where your circuit breaker box is located. Make sure it's easy to access and that the circuits are labeled correctly. This will save you from unnecessary frustration when you are trying to turn the power off in a specific room or appliance."

—Erica Catherman

Find a Stud in the Wall

YOU WILL NEED:
- Blank wall
- Electronic stud finder
- Pencil or tape
- Knuckles

TIME REQUIRED:
30 seconds

*P*utting a hole or a nail in the wall? You may want to find the stud in the wall. What's a stud, you ask? A stud is one board of the structural framing within a wall. In essence, a stud is part of the skeleton of a structure. Knowing where studs are is helpful if you plan on changing the structure or would like to hang a heavy object on your wall. By hanging something heavy on a stud, you may avoid said object hitting the floor—Sheetrock alone can't always hold what you want to hang.

STEP 1

Prep the stud finder. Turn the stud finder on and set it flush against the wall. Activate the detection button on the stud finder to initiate the stud sensor.

291

Guesstimate. Studs are generally set about 16″ apart "on center" (from one stud's center to the next). About where you hope to find a stud, slide the stud finder on the wall in either direction. When the sensor locates a stud, it will alert you with a light, beeping, or both.

Mark the stud. When you have located a stud, mark the approximate center of the stud with a pencil line or tape. Knock on the wall and listen for a solid sound behind the Sheetrock.

Did You Know?

There are two primary types of stud finders: (1) an electronic one detects differences in the wall's density to identify a wooden beam within the wall; and (2) a magnetic detector finds metal studs, and some screws or nails in wooden studs.

Hang a Picture

<table>
<tr><td>YOU WILL NEED:</td><td>TIME REQUIRED:</td></tr>
<tr><td>• Hammer   • Stud finder
• Nail   • Framed picture</td><td>2 minutes</td></tr>
</table>

*D*ecorating a space with stuff you like can be fun. It's a way to show what you like and surround yourself with the images and things you enjoy. Most colleges don't allow you to put nails in the walls of your dorm room. But there are products to help you with that. Once you are allowed to hang pictures for real, you should know how!

STEP **1**

Find the stud. Use a stud finder to locate a solid place to hammer in the picture-hanging nail. (See "How to Find a Stud in the Wall.")

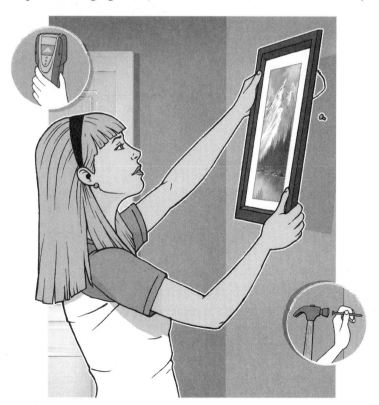

Hammer the nail. Gently and precisely drive a nail into the wall. Leave ¾ of an inch extending out from the wall to hang the picture on. (See "How to Swing a Hammer.")

Hang the picture. Lower the wire or hanging clasp down onto the nail. Use your visually keen eye or level tool to align the picture to level. (See "How to Use a Level.")

Did You Know?

Leonardo da Vinci's *Mona Lisa* is acclaimed to be "the best known, the most visited, the most written about, the most sung about, the most parodied work of art in the world."[4] Painted in the early 1500s, the framed smiling lady has gained great value in the past 500 years. Today she is estimated to be worth approximately $760,000,000. That's one expensive piece of art hanging on the wall.

Fix a Small Hole in a Wall

YOU WILL NEED:

- Small can of spackling
- 1½″ putty knife
- Fine-weight sand-paper (120-grit)
- Paint to match wall color
- Paintbrush

TIME REQUIRED:

1 minute prep, 30 minutes dry

*W*hile moving furniture in your room you accidently put a small hole in the wall. Who knew Sheetrock crushed so easily? Not a problem. Once you are done redecorating, return to the hole for a quick spackle fix. Your place will be looking good again in no time.

STEP **1**

Prepare hole. Carefully remove any chunks of broken drywall.

Spread spackling. Use the end of your finger or putty knife to spread spackling into the small hole. Spread spackling beyond the edge of the hole and so that it rises out farther than the surface of the surrounding wall.

Let dry. Wait until the spackling is fully dry. Some spackling slowly turns from an application color to white, which is an indicator that the product is dry.

Sand patch. Swipe the sandpaper over the dried spackling to knock the texture down to the same level as the surrounding wall.

Repeat if needed. If the spackling dried lower than the surrounding wall, clean the area free of dust, add another layer of spackling, let dry, and re-sand.

Touch up. Paint your patch to match the surrounding wall color.

Fact or Fiction:

Toothpaste makes for a quick-fix spackling.

Fact. Yet anything larger than a nail hole is too big to brush up with toothpaste. Gear up and fix it right or call in a professional.

Notes

Part 1 Guys & Dating

1. Rosalie Maggio, *The Beacon Book of Quotations by Women* (Boston: Beacon Press, 1992), 130.
2. John Medina, *Brain Rules* (Seattle: Pear Press, 2008), 253–54.

Part 2 Social Skills & Manners

1. http://emilypost.com/aboutemily-postquotations.
2. Press conference, New Delhi (October 19, 1971), quoted in Sydney H. Schanberg, "Indian and Pakistani Armies Confront Each Other Along Borders," *New York Times* (October 20, 1971), 6C.

Part 3 Work & Ethics

1. "Exclusive: First Lady Michelle Obama on Being Successful & Having It All," Sophia A. Nelson, *Essence*, June, 29, 2012, https://www.essence.com/2012/07/01/.
2. Erica Catherman interview with Georgia Kruger, November 29, 2017.
3. Oprah Winfrey, "What I Know for Sure," Oprah.com, http://www.oprah.com/omagazine /what-i-know-for-sure-hard-work.
4. Katharine Whitehorn, as quoted in Roger Shelby, *The Executive's Lifetime Library of Model Speeches for Every Situation* (Armock, NY: M. E. Sharpe, 1998), 271.
5. Barbara Corcoran, Twitter post, @BarbaraCorcoran, September 21, 2016, 12:05 p.m.

Part 4 Wealth & Money Management

1. https://www.rachelcruze.com/about.
2. Rachel Cruze, "4 Common Sense Money Habits for Everyday Living," https://www .youtube.com/watch?v=z-jG4y748UA.
3. Cruze, "4 Common Sense Money Habits."
4. Dave Ramsey, Twitter post, @DaveRamsey, May 20, 2014, 4:16 a.m.
5. Rachel Cruze, RachelCruze.com, Debt-Free Living section, "The Power of Compound Interest," https://www.rachelcruze.com/topics/debt-free-living/the-power-of-compound -interest-will-blow-your-mind.
6. Suze's Daily Inspiration, January 11, 2018, https://www.suzeorman.com.

Part 5 Health & Beauty

1. Erica Catherman interview with Kelly Grathwohl, August 21, 2017.
2. John Medina, *Brain Rules* (Seattle: Pear Press, 2008), 10–11.

Part 6 Clothes & Fashion

1. Maya Angelou's Facebook page, July 4, 2011, https://www.facebook.com/MayaAngelou/posts/10150251846629796.
2. Kate Spade, as quoted in Jackie Walker and Pamela Dittmer McKuen, *Expressionista: How to Express Your True Self Through (and Despite) Fashion* (New York: Simon and Schuster, 2013), 65.
3. http://anneklein.com/then/.
4. Coco Chanel, as quoted in *Architectural Digest*, September 1994, 30.

Part 7 Sports & Recreation

1. Erica Catherman interview with Megan Manthey, August 18, 2017.
2. Catherman interview with Manthey.
3. Annika Sorenstam, as quoted in Mandy Antoniacci, "10 Empowering Leadership Quotes From Women's Golf," Inc.com, June 11, 2015, https://www.inc.com/mandy-antoniacci/10-empowering-quotes-for-female-leaders-from-condoleezza-rice-and-the-lpga.html.

Part 8 Cars & Driving

1. Erica Catherman interview with Allison Bormann, August 29, 2017.
2. National Association for Stock Car Auto Racing.
3. The National Auto Sport Association.
4. Sports Car Club of America.
5. Catherman interview with Bormann.

Part 9 Food & Cooking

1. http://www.pbs.org/food/features/julia-child-quotes/.
2. Erica Catherman interview with Stacey Coates, August 16, 2017.
3. Erica Catherman interview with Britten Shelson, August 16, 2017.
4. http://www.harpersbazaar.com/fashion/photography/a606/katy-perry-interview-1210
5. Julia Child, as quoted by Katie Workman, "Fifteen Julia Child Quotes That Inspire the Wannabe Chef in All of Us," Today.com, Aug. 15, 2016, https://www.today.com/food/15-julia-child-quotes-inspire-wannabe-chef-all-us-t101848.

Part 10 Tools & Fit-It

1. Erica Catherman interview with Emily Pilloton, August 29, 2017.
2. https://science.howstuffworks.com/innovation/inventions/10-things-that-women-invented1.htm.
3. Kimberly Wang, "HGTV's Nicole Curtis Shares Must-Know Tips for First-Time Home DIYers," Brit.co, Oct. 30, 2015 (updated Jan. 20, 2016), https://www.brit.co/nicole-curtis-rehab-addict-hgtv/.
4. John Lichfield, "The Moving of the Mona Lisa," *The Independent*, Apr. 1, 2005 (retrieved March 9, 2012), http://www.independent.co.uk/news/world/europe/the-moving-of-the-mona-lisa-530771.html.

Erica Catherman has spent more than twenty years mentoring young women as a coach to middle school, high school, and college students. Committed to raising up the next generation to be kind, confident, and capable, Erica has served as a youth group leader, community volunteer, and advocate for gender equality in sports. She is a certified Yoga Alliance and Group Fitness instructor.

Jonathan Catherman is the author of the bestselling *The Manual to Manhood* and *The Manual to Middle School*. An award-winning cultural strategist and a leading education trainer specializing in the character and leadership development of youth, Jonathan speaks worldwide about the principles and strengths that empower greatness in children, teens, and young adults.

Erica and Jonathan live in North Carolina, working together to raise a family that includes two teenagers and a couple of big dogs. Learn more at www.TheCathermans.com.

100 DO'S AND DON'TS
FOR NAVIGATING MIDDLE SCHOOL

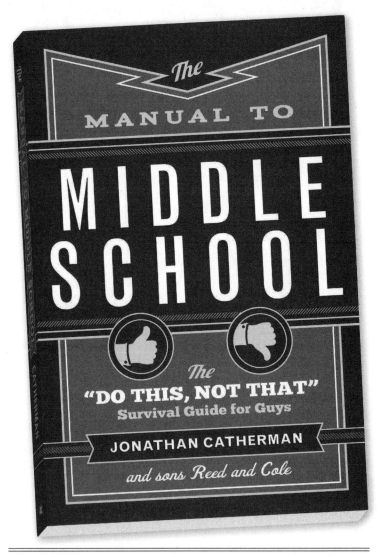

With real-life hacks, humorous illustrations, and tons of true survival stories, Jonathan Catherman and his sons, Reed and Cole, will get you through middle school like a pro.